STUDENT UNIT GUIDE

NEW EDITION

OCR AS Business Studies Unit F292

Business Functions

Andy Mottershead, Judith Kelt
and Alex Grant

PHILIP ALLAN

Philip Allan, an imprint of Hodder Education, an Hachette UK company, Market Place, Deddington, Oxfordshire OX15 0SE

Orders
Bookpoint Ltd, 130 Milton Park, Abingdon, Oxfordshire OX14 4SB
tel: 01235 827827
fax: 01235 400401
e-mail: education@bookpoint.co.uk
Lines are open 9.00 a.m.–5.00 p.m., Monday to Saturday, with a 24-hour message answering service.
You can also order through the Philip Allan website: www.philipallan.co.uk

ISBN 978-1-4441-7197-6

First printed 2012
Impression number 5 4 3 2 1
Year 2016 2015 2014 2013 2012

Cover photo: Eric Middelkoop/Fotolia

Typeset by Integra Software Services Pvt. Ltd., Pondicherry, India

Printed in Dubai

Hachette UK's policy is to use papers that are natural, renewable and recyclable products and made from wood grown in sustainable forests. The logging and manufacturing processes are expected to conform to the environmental regulations of the country of origin.

P2093

Contents

Content Guidance

Question & Answers

Getting the most from this book

Questions & Answers

Exam-style questions

Examiner comments on the questions

Tips on what you need to do to gain full marks, indicated by the icon e.

Sample student answers

Practise the questions, then look at the student answers that follow each set of questions.

Perry and Joseph Cottages | Case study

(5) Discuss the most appropriate methods of motivating the company's staff in a more effective manner.
(20 marks)

It is important to note that the question asks you to consider the 'most appropriate methods'. It also asks you to think about motivating the staff in a 'more effective manner'. Therefore your answer will need to explain what criteria you are using for 'effective'. Effectiveness might involve being cost-effective, or successfully motivating the staff and helping to improve the quality of their work. It might also mean that the level of absenteeism falls. Therefore when considering the various approaches, you will need to think about how the employees at P&J can be motivated and then try to justify your observations with references to the theories of motivation. A poor answer may just list the theories. A good answer will apply certain selected theories, appropriate for P&J, and show the implications of using them and how they will hopefully improve motivation in an effective way.

Total for Section B: 72 marks
Overall total: 90 marks

Student A

Section A

(1) (a) 2 types of objectives are tactical and strategic.

2/2 marks awarded. Correct answer, although there is no need to write out part of the question.

(b) Current liabilities are an overdraft and creditors.

2/2 marks awarded.

(c) On-the-job training takes place whilst at work and is usually done by other employees who have the experience and time.

2/2 marks awarded. The student has correctly shown that it takes place at work and who does the training. It could be done by an outside agency as well.

(d) 15,000 × 100 ÷ 20%
75,000

4/4 marks awarded. Some workings have been shown. Although the student does not show how the 75,000 was reached, this does not matter provided the sum is correct. A clear layout to help the examiner is to be encouraged.

(e) Two styles of leadership are autocratic and democratic. a An autocratic leader makes all the decisions and does not involve the workers. This type of leader is centralised. b A democratic leader involves the workers so they are more motivated. c

4/4 marks awarded. a Level 1 marks — the student shows knowledge of leadership styles. b This is sufficient to show an understanding, especially the comment on the lack of employee involvement, and would gain Level 2 marks. (The comment on centralisation is on the right lines.)

Unit F292: Business Functions

Examiner commentary on sample student answers

Find out how many marks each answer would be awarded in the exam and then read the examiner comments (preceded by the icon e) following each student answer. Annotations that link back to points made in the student answers show exactly how and where marks are gained or lost.

About this book

The aim of this guide is to help you to maximise your grade in the OCR examination: Business Functions (Unit F292). The information contained in the guide has been organised to mirror the textbook, *OCR AS Business Studies* (2nd edition) by Andy Mottershead, Steve Challoner and Alex Grant. This order reflects the order of the topics within the OCR specification. If you have not got a copy of the specification, it is worth downloading from the OCR website (www.ocr.org.uk), as you will then be able to tick off the topics as your revision progresses.

The guide is divided into two main sections to make your revision easier.

- **Content Guidance.** This section, which closely follows the OCR specification, outlines all the topics on which you may be tested in the examination.
- **Questions and Answers.** In this section there are two case studies for you to attempt. Each case study is very similar to what you can expect to see in your final examination. They contain the same number and type of questions as the examination to enable you to become familiar with the format of the paper. Sample A-grade answers are included to help you see what is required to reach this grade. Examiner's comments explain how each student answer is awarded marks, and highlight the exact point at which a particular level is awarded, so that you can quickly and easily adopt a similar strategy in your answers. The comments also indicate why some students fall short of an A grade.

Content Guidance

Marketing

Marketing objectives and strategy

Marketing objectives

These are objectives set by the marketing department in the overall strategy of the business. The **strategic objectives** that apply particularly to marketing are:

- increasing sales
- increasing market share
- increasing price awareness
- gaining a unique selling point

The **tactical objectives** fall into the four sections of the marketing mix.

Product objectives

- launch of new products
- product improvement
- improvements in after-sales service
- improvements or changes in packaging
- extension strategies in the product life cycle

Price objectives

- remaining competitive
- introducing new pricing strategies
- reducing price while remaining competitive

Promotion objectives

- to maintain brand awareness
- to increase brand loyalty
- to develop effective advertising
- to increase the promotional methods

Place objectives

- to increase product availability
- to improve delivery times
- to consider new methods of distribution

Marketing strategy

This can also be looked at in terms of the marketing mix.

Knowledge check 1

State three ways in which marketing activities help a business.

OCR AS Business Studies

Product strategy

- the need to update the range of products
- market research to assess consumer demand
- monitoring after-sales service and customer satisfaction
- working with the production department on product development
- price strategy
- the need to remain competitive
- awareness of competition
- awareness of the market and the economy

Promotion strategy

- raising the profile of the product
- preparing a range of promotional activities
- launching new products

Place strategy

- choice of distribution method
- the impact of the distribution method on other aspects of the marketing mix

Examiner tip
Always think of marketing in terms of the four Ps — product, price, promotion and place.

Market research strategy

In addition, businesses need to consider the methods of market research they are going to use before putting all the other strategies in place. The business needs to:

- adopt a strategic approach
- consider the whole picture
- review the process constantly to check that it is working well
- learn from experience
- consider the changing business and economic environment
- pay attention to the resources that are available (e.g. the marketing budget)
- establish a unique selling point — this is one of the most important factors in the whole process

Analysis

It is possible to analyse a situation from the point of view of what the business can do, in terms of marketing, to increase sales or profit. For example, the business could consider a promotional strategy in order to improve product awareness and sales, and therefore profits.

Evaluation

Evaluation marks can be achieved by discussing which part of the marketing mix might be most likely to increase sales and profits. For example, the business could introduce a new pricing policy to take business away from competitors and improve its performance in the long term.

Marketing

What is marketing?

Marketing involves:

- **Identifying customer demand.** Business is concerned with supplying something that consumers want to buy. Businesses find out what consumers want through market research.
- **Satisfying customer demand.** The business then needs to match supply to the demands of the market. In doing this, it may need to convince consumers that they want to buy a particular product through appropriate promotional and pricing strategies.
- **Making a profit.** Most firms want to make a profit or avoid making a loss as a consequence of trading.

Marketing comprises all of these elements, not just one of them.

Marketing is usually studied in terms of four elements known together as the **marketing mix**. These elements, also known as the **four Ps**, are product, price, promotion and place.

Customer or product orientation

Firms have traditionally adopted two approaches to marketing:

- A **customer orientation** means that the business provides what the customer wants to buy. The increase in production of organic foods is a result of changes in consumer demand.
- A **product orientation** means that the business develops a product that it hopes the consumer can be persuaded to buy. Firms producing mobile phones are continually pushing technological boundaries to introduce phones with new features.

Knowledge check 2

Give an example of a business that is likely to be product orientated.

Relationship between marketing and other business functions

Marketing is only one part of the business organisation. It must be seen as an integral part of the business and not in isolation from other aspects of it.

The marketing department needs to be aware of the constraints that come from other parts of the business. At times, conflict may arise with other departments:

- **Accounting and finance departments.** These may come into conflict with marketing if they are attempting to control costs. The costs of promotion in any business can be considerable.
- **Human resource department.** Marketing departments hope to introduce new products and create more demand. This creates the need for training and change among the workforce. Failure to create demand is likely to result in redundancies.
- **Production department.** This needs to coordinate its operation with the marketing department. Marketing needs to work alongside production to ensure that the products it hopes to sell can be delivered by the production department.

Each part of the business has different priorities. Conflict is more likely to arise when the business is struggling than when it is successful.

Analysis

Analysis could be achieved by discussing the benefits of having a customer or product orientation in terms of improving sales and increasing profit for the business.

Evaluation

This could involve a discussion about whether it is better for the business to pursue a product or customer orientation in order to improve the business's long-term performance.

Examiner tip

It is important to think of marketing in a whole business context — there will always be cost and production implications when making marketing decisions.

Market segmentation, share and growth

Market segmentation

Market segmentation means identifying a specific group within the total market. It has several benefits:
- This group can be targeted with promotional campaigns.
- Market research can be used to find out more about the segment.
- The product can be differentiated to suit the tastes of the segment.
- Gaps in the market can be identified and niches found.

Types of market segmentation
- **Geographical.** This means dividing the market according to where people live. For example, sales of meat pies are higher in the north of England and Scotland than in the south of England.
- **Lifestyle.** This means dividing people according to their leisure pursuits and hobbies. For example, demand for cruises has increased among retired people in recent years.
- **Age.** This is one of the main methods of segmentation. For example, a number of specialist firms now provide gap-year holidays for students.
- **Gender.** Many products are aimed at either males or females. For example, some car models are aimed specifically at one gender or the other.
- **Social class.** Social class is often categorised using government class listings. These put people into groups such as professionals, junior management and unskilled workers. The groups are given letters: A — upper class (professionals); B — middle class (middle management); C1 — lower middle class (junior management); C2 — skilled working class (tradespeople); D — working class (unskilled manual workers); E — unskilled/unemployed.
- **Residence.** This form of segmentation categorises people by the type of house they live in. The system is called ACORN (A Classification of Residential

Neighbourhoods). A private school might use such a system to send out advertising literature to the families of potential students.
- **Behaviour.** This categorises customers by their spending habits. A business like B&Q might have '10% off' days for retired customers.

Niche marketing

Niche marketing is marketing to a specific, and often small, market segment. Examples of niche markets are Morgan Cars and escorted historical holidays.

Niche marketing has the following features:
- There are usually fewer competitors.
- There may still be economies of scale if there are no other competitors.
- Smaller markets have less scope for profit in most cases.
- It may also be dangerous to rely on a small market.
- Others may be encouraged to enter if the market yields success.

Product differentiation

Product differentiation involves encouraging consumers to see the product as different from those of competitors. Some consumers, for example, will always buy a particular brand of chocolate.
- The differences may be real or imaginary, reinforced by advertising.
- Consumers may be prepared to pay premiums for their preferred products (e.g. branded sportswear).

Market share

Market share is the proportion of the total market that is controlled by the business. It can be measured by sales revenue or volume.

The formula for market share is:

$$\text{market share} = \frac{\text{sales value or volume for the product or business}}{\text{total sales value or volume for the whole market}} \times 100\%$$

Example: sales of local sandwich bar in a town = £500

total sales of sandwiches in the town = £2,500

$$\text{market share} = \frac{500}{2,500} \times 100\% = 20\%$$

Market share can be used to measure the success of a business. It can also be used to measure its size.

Market growth

A growth in the size of a market can have a big impact on a firm's success, even if its share of the market remains unchanged.

The factors contributing to market growth are:
- **The type of product.** Firms in the technology sector achieve rapid growth in the market for their products in the early months after launch.

- **Changes in tastes and fashions.** The clothing industry experiences rapid growth in sales at the beginning of each season.
- **Standard of living.** As people become better off, firms producing at the luxury end of the market are likely to experience growth.
- **Social and demographic changes.** The market for products like stair lifts will grow as the number of elderly people in the population rises.

The formula for market growth is:

$$\text{market growth} = \frac{\text{increase in sales for the market in a period of time}}{\text{sales at the beginning of the period}} \times 100\%$$

Example: sales in 2011 = 60,000 units

sales in 2012 = 66,000 units

$$\text{market growth} = \frac{66,000 - 60,000}{60,000} \times 100$$

$$= \frac{6,000}{60,000} \times 100 = 10\%$$

Knowledge of market share and market growth is useful in predicting future trends more accurately.

Knowledge check 4

Explain the difference between market share and market growth.

Analysis

Knowledge of market segmentation makes it possible for the business to target specific customers with promotion and therefore increases the likelihood of higher sales and profits.

Evaluation

Evaluation marks can be achieved by discussing the best way for the business to segment its market and to target segments with promotional strategies.

Products

What is a product?

- The term **product** can refer to a good or a service.
- Product is one aspect of the marketing mix.
- Good products perform and look as the consumer expects and can be sold at a profit.
- The process by which firms assess the performance and design of their products to ensure that they meet consumers' expectations is called **value analysis**.

Marketing models

Marketing models are useful in helping a firm to assess its current performance and plan its strategies for the future.

Product life cycle

This model assumes that all products follow the same cycle in their pattern of sales.

The time taken to pass through the life cycle varies by product. Women's clothing has a short life cycle; many food products, such as Kellogg's Cornflakes, have long life cycles.

The stages of the life cycle, shown in Figure 1, are as follows:

(1) Introduction. The product is put on to the market.

(2) Growth. The market for the product increases through the use of promotion.

(3) Maturity. Profits are maximised at this stage. Some products, such as Mars Bars, have been at this stage for many years. **Extension strategies** can be introduced at this stage.

(4) Decline. Sales begin to fall. New versions can be introduced.

The product life cycle can be used to assess the need for marketing strategies.

Knowledge check 5

Give an example of an extension strategy that a business may use.

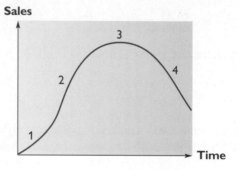

Figure 1 The product life cycle

Product portfolio analysis

This model allows a firm to assess where its products are currently in the market.

The **Boston matrix** (see Figure 2) is the best-known technique of product portfolio analysis. Products are assessed according to their market share in a high- or low-growing total market situation.

Examiner tip

Ensure that you can draw the Boston matrix diagram accurately, including the labels on the sides.

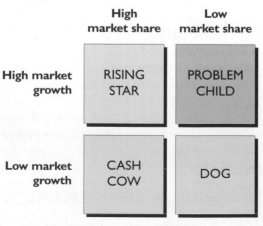

Figure 2 The Boston matrix

The four elements of the Boston matrix are:
- **Rising star.** This is a product with a high market share in a fast-growing market. Promotion is needed to maintain market share and to fight off competition.
- **Cash cow.** This is a product with a high market share in a slow-growing market. Reminder advertising is needed to maintain consumer awareness.
- **Problem child.** This is a product with a low market share in a rapidly growing market. Market research may be needed to find out why market share is low. There are opportunities for growth of sales in such a market.
- **Dog.** This is a product with a low share of a slow-growing market. There may be little future scope for such a product unless extension strategies can be found.

Analysis

It is possible to achieve analysis by considering the ways in which the business can increase the life of its product, or move it from being a 'problem child' to a 'rising star', for example. This will then enable the business to increase its market share for this product.

Evaluation

Evaluation can be achieved by discussing the best way for the business to market its product in terms of the market in which it competes and the current stage of the product life cycle.

Knowledge check 6

Why might a company continue to sell a 'problem child' product?

Price

Price is the second element of the marketing mix. It allows the consumer to decide whether the product represents value for money.

What determines price?

Price is determined by:
- price elasticity of demand (see p. 18)
- demand for the product — the higher the demand, the higher the price
- product quality
- the pricing strategy used by the firm
- competitors' prices

Examiner tip

Do not confuse price and costs in your answers. Price is the amount paid by the consumer to the supplier for goods and services. Costs are the outgoings of the business to purchase things like raw materials and to pay the wages for labour.

Pricing strategies

- **Cost plus pricing.** This involves the business working out the cost of producing one unit of the product and then adding a percentage for profit. It is sometimes called mark-up pricing. It is simple to use and ensures that a profit is made. If the cost of producing a unit is £6 and the mark-up is to be 200%, then £12 will be added on to the cost. This will give a price of £18.
- **Contribution pricing.** Here the price is set to ensure that the variable costs of production are met. Any extra will be a contribution to the company's fixed costs or overheads (see p. 24), e.g. if the variable cost of producing a doll is £12 and its sale price is £25, the contribution to overheads from each doll produced is £13.

Examiner tip

Remember that demand and supply interact through price — not directly. Changes in demand or supply affect price first. This then leads to a change in supply or demand.

- **Price discrimination.** This involves charging different prices to different groups of consumers for the same service. It is used extensively in the transport and telephone industries, where discrimination is usually by time of day.
- **Promotional pricing.** This is used extensively by the supermarket sector. It may involve an introductory offer or a special promotion.
- **Psychological pricing.** This is using prices such as £9.99 to try to convince consumers that they are paying less.
- **Price skimming.** This strategy is often used by technology businesses when they introduce a new product. They begin by charging a high price to recover their research and development costs. Those who are keen to buy the latest games console, for example, will be prepared to pay this price. Over time, the price will be gradually reduced to appeal to a mass market.
- **Penetration pricing.** This involves introducing a new product at a lower price than will eventually be the case. Collectors' magazines use this technique for the first issue of a series to try to encourage consumers to continue buying the whole series when the price rises.
- **Loss leading.** This involves selling one product at a loss to encourage the consumer into the shop and increase sales of other products. It is often used by supermarkets for essential goods, such as bread.
- **Predatory/destroyer pricing.** This strategy may be used by large firms to try to force smaller competitors out of business. It may be used by some supermarkets when they open a new store in a new location.

Selecting the right method

This is an important strategic decision for a business. Choosing the right pricing method is vital in attracting and keeping consumers in the short and the long term. Consumers are much more aware of prices than used to be the case because of the widespread use of the internet and comparison websites.

Analysis

Analysis marks can be achieved by a discussion of the firm adopting a particular pricing strategy. The discussion should be of the kind: 'if the firm adopts this pricing strategy, it will result in an increase in sales and an improvement in profit'.

Evaluation

Evaluation can be achieved by discussing the best pricing strategy for the business in its current circumstances and given its current competition.

Distribution

Place, as one of the four Ps in the marketing mix, refers to distribution — the methods by which the business gets the product to the consumer.

Physical distribution

Physical distribution is the physical movement of goods. The internet has led to an increase in distribution by post and delivery service, direct to the customer. For many firms, distribution involves transportation worldwide.

Channels of distribution

These are chains of intermediaries. The intermediaries are:

- **Wholesalers.** Wholesalers act as a link between producers and retailers. They break bulk into smaller and more manageable quantities, and are used particularly by restaurants, public houses and small local shops.
- **Retailers.** Retailers sell direct to the consumer. They may vary in size from small shops to large retailers like Tesco and Marks and Spencer.
- **Agents.** Agents provide a link between sellers and buyers. They never own the product that they are selling. They are usually paid commission on sales, and are found in sectors like travel, house sales and the import/export sector.

Common channels of distribution are shown in Figure 3.

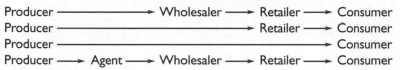

Figure 3 Common channels of distribution

Factors affecting distribution

Distribution is affected by the following factors:

- **Cost.** A business will want to find the shortest possible channel to keep the costs as low as possible.
- **Type of product.** The nature of the product is important. Perishable goods, such as bread and milk, need to be delivered quickly; heavy products, like bricks, will usually go straight to the building site.
- **Type of firm.** Larger companies increasingly distribute directly, cutting out wholesalers. Waitrose's delivery service, Ocado, delivers straight from a central warehouse to the customer's home.
- **Spread of the market.** This depends on the product and the size of the business. A solicitor is likely to serve a local area, whereas a business like Cadbury will distribute worldwide.
- **Control required by the producer.** Some producers may prefer to sell direct to their customers so that they can keep control of how their products are marketed. Most Dell computers are sold direct rather than through retail outlets.

Ensuring good links with intermediaries

Producers who rely on intermediaries to sell their products will try to provide a variety of marketing services to help promote the product. These might include:

- specific product displays, including equipment such as fridges and freezers
- competitions for retailers, offering them prizes for achieving sales targets

Physical distribution
The way in which goods are transported between different intermediaries, e.g. the mode of transport used.

Knowledge check 8

Give two ways in which the channels of distribution from producer to consumer have changed in the last 20 years.

- special deals on products or commission on sales
- training for retailers, particularly on the technical aspects of a product

Analysis

Analysis marks can be achieved by discussing how the firm could benefit by adopting a particular method of distribution. New methods of distribution could improve efficiency and reduce costs.

Evaluation

Evaluation can be shown by discussing the best method of evaluation for the business, taking into account the product it offers, the nature of the consumer and the type of competition.

Promotion

What is promotion?

Promotion is not just advertising.
- It can be **informative**, giving the consumer more information about the nature of the product.
- It can be **persuasive** by portraying the advantages of purchasing the product.

Methods of promotion

Above-the-line promotion

Above-the-line promotion This utilises mass media to reach a wide audience.

Above-the-line promotion makes use of mass media to target the audience.
- **Television advertising.** This form of advertising is very expensive and consequently can only be used by larger firms. It is able to reach a mass market audience. However, some potential customers may not be watching, and many people who are watching may not be interested in the product.
- **Newspaper advertising.** This method can be used to target more specific groups according to the paper they read. It is good for relaying more complex information and the reader can always refer back to it.
- **Radio advertising.** This has increased in popularity as the number of radio channels has increased. It is useful for targeting specific demographic groups. For example, Classic FM often carries adverts for financial products to fit its listener base.
- **Magazine advertising.** This is also good for targeting specific demographic groups. As with newspapers, the reader can always refer back to the advert.
- **Electronic advertising.** This has increased as use of the internet and mobile phones has risen. It is another good method for targeting specific demographic or special interest groups.
- **Billboard advertising.** This method can give a relatively small amount of information, but it will reach a large target audience, whether it be for a television programme or the school open day.
- **Cinema advertising.** Once again, this method can be used to target the audience, depending on the particular film that is being shown.

Below-the-line promotion

Below-the-line promotion is targeted more closely at a potential market segment.

- **Personal selling.** This involves a personal approach to the customer by sales staff. It may be on the phone, at the door or in the office.
- **Sales promotions.** Many such methods are used by businesses. They include buy one, get one free; gifts; introductory offers; and money-off coupons.
- **Competitions.** These help to increase demand by offering high-profile prizes.
- **Trade fairs and exhibitions.** Some businesses rely heavily on trade fairs to encourage demand. A local florist may generate new business by attending wedding fairs in local hotels.
- **Sponsorship.** Many firms gain publicity by sponsoring events or teams. These might be large scale, such as the sponsorship of a Premiership football team, or small scale, such as the sponsorship of a school netball team.
- **Publicity.** This is a method of portraying the business in a positive light through press reports. A sponsored run by local bank employees reported in the newspaper is an example.

Which method of promotion to choose?

The decision may depend on one or more of the following factors:

- **Nature of the product being sold.** Specialist model-making equipment will be promoted in magazines targeted at this hobby.
- **Timescale.** Some products, such as television programmes, need to be advertised for a short time.
- **Finance available.** This is the major constraint for most firms. The budget for promotion and advertising determines what can be done.
- **Type of customer.** It is very important that the method used takes into account the lifestyle of the potential user and whether they will see the promotion.
- **External influences.** This will include factors like new technology and government legislation on advertising.

Analysis

You can show analysis by discussing the effects of a particular type of promotional strategy on the sales and profits of the business.

Evaluation

Evaluation marks can be achieved by discussing the best way for the business to promote its product, given the nature of the product, the type of consumer and the competition in the market.

Elasticity of demand

Elasticity of demand measures the extent to which demand changes following a change in price.

Below-the-line promotion This targets specific customers directly.

Knowledge check 9

Give two examples of above-the-line promotion.

Examiner tip

Make sure that the method of promotion you choose or suggest is appropriate to the particular firm. Small businesses will not be able to advertise on the television or in the national press. They could not afford it and it would not be an effective way to reach their target market.

Price elasticity of demand

Price elasticity of demand measures how much demand changes when the price changes.

The normal law of demand states that when price falls, demand will rise for a normal good. Price elasticity of demand tells you by how much it will rise.

The formula for measuring price elasticity (PED) is:

$$\text{PED} = \frac{\text{percentage change in quantity demanded}}{\text{percentage change in price}}$$

Examiner tip

Make sure you get the numbers the right way round. Quantity change on top; price change underneath.

Example

The demand for flat-screen televisions rises from 1,000 to 1,500 per week when their price falls from £500 to £400.

$$\text{percentage change in demand} = \frac{(1{,}500 - 1{,}000)}{1{,}000} \times 100 = \frac{500}{1{,}000} \times 100 = 50\%$$

$$\text{percentage change in price} = \frac{(500 - 400)}{500} \times 100 = \frac{100}{500} \times 100 = 20\%$$

$$\text{PED} = \frac{50}{20} = 2.5$$

If the value for price elasticity is greater than 1, demand is said to be elastic. This means that demand is responsive to price changes. If the value for price elasticity is less than 1, demand is said to be inelastic. This means that demand is not very responsive to price changes.

The same rules and formula will apply whether the price rises or falls.

- Goods that have elastic demand are likely to be luxuries and/or have good substitutes (e.g. beef, strawberries).
- Goods that have inelastic demand are likely to be necessities and/or not have good substitutes (e.g. salt, bread).

Examiner tip

Ensure that you can define elasticity clearly. It is the *extent* by which demand changes, not whether demand goes up or down.

Brand loyalty may also reduce elasticity.

Is price elasticity useful?

A knowledge of elasticity helps to inform a business about the result of raising or lowering prices.

- If a product has elastic demand, a price rise will lower the firm's total revenue; there will be a larger percentage fall in demand than the rise in price.
- If a product has elastic demand, a price fall will increase total revenue. There will be larger percentage rise in demand than the fall in price.
- If a product has inelastic demand, a price rise will increase total revenue; there will be a smaller percentage fall in demand than the rise in price.
- If a product has inelastic demand, a price fall will reduce total revenue; there will be a smaller percentage rise in demand than the fall in price.

Knowledge check 10

What characteristics would you expect to find in a product that has inelastic demand?

Other types of elasticity

Income elasticity of demand is the responsiveness of demand to changes in income. The formula is:

$$\text{income elasticity of demand} = \frac{\text{percentage change in quantity demanded}}{\text{percentage change in income}}$$

Advertising elasticity of demand is the responsiveness of demand to advertising spending. The formula is:

$$\text{advertising elasticity of demand} = \frac{\text{percentage change in quantity demanded}}{\text{percentage change in advertising spending}}$$

Analysis

It is easy to achieve analysis marks in a discussion of elasticity. The discussion needs to centre on whether demand is elastic or inelastic and whether it is a good idea to raise or lower prices in those circumstances.

Evaluation

Evaluation will then come from discussing the best course of action for the business, given the elasticity situation that it faces.

Summary

- A firm's marketing objectives may be strategic, like increasing sales or market share. They may also be based around the four Ps: product, price, promotion and place.
- Firms need to establish a unique selling point for their products, if possible. Marketing involves identifying consumer demand, satisfying it and making a profit in the process.
- Marketing departments cannot work in isolation. They need to take financial, human resource and production constraints into account.
- Firms segment their markets to try to identify particular characteristics of segments so that they can meet their demands more specifically.
- Niche marketing targets a small section of a market as opposed to mass marketing.
- Market share is the proportion of a market that a firm has achieved.
- Market growth is an increase in the total market demand.
- Product — businesses must ensure that their product meets the demands of the consumer if they are to be successful.
- The product life cycle explains the development of a product in its market from the development to the decline stage.
- The Boston matrix identifies different types of products in terms of market share and the growth of the market.
- Price is a significant factor in determining the success of a product.
- Firms can use different pricing strategies — contribution, cost plus, price discrimination, psychological, predatory, loss leading, price skimming, price penetration.
- Distribution channels have changed considerably in recent years.
- Physical distribution is the type of transport that is used, e.g. road transport.

(Summary continues over the page)

Summary

(Continued)

- The intermediaries in the distribution channel are wholesalers, retailers, agents and the consumer.
- Promotion can be above the line or below the line.
- The method of promotion chosen will depend on the type of business, its size, the budget available and the type of customer.

- Price elasticity of demand is the extent to which demand changes following a change in price. If it is less than 1 the product has inelastic demand; if it is more than 1, demand is elastic.
- Goods with inelastic demand are usually necessities or products with no close substitute.
- It is useful for businesses to know the elasticity they face when it comes to changing price.

Accounting and finance

Budgets

The purpose of budgets

A **budget** is a forecast of future income or expenditure. It usually operates within the period of 1 year.

The budget serves many functions:
- a measure to check progress or success
- useful for controlling expenditure
- can aid efficiency
- provides a target
- gives an opportunity for departments to take responsibility for running their own budgets

Knowledge check 11

State two functions of a budget.

Limitations of budgets

- Budgets are only useful if there is a degree of realism. Setting unrealistic budgets can be counterproductive.
- Setting a realistic budget for a new business is difficult as there are no previous figures to use as a guide.
- Circumstances in the business environment can change very quickly.
- The actual process of setting budgets is time-consuming.

Variance

Variance is the difference between forecast (budgeted) and actual figures. For example, if forecast sales are 500 sales and actual sales are 600, the variance is +100. When the actual value is greater than the budgeted value, the variance is positive.

A variance can also be calculated as a percentage:

$$\text{sales variance} = \frac{100}{500} \times 100 = 20\% \text{ (positive)}$$

(The terms 'favourable' and 'adverse' may be used instead of 'negative' and 'positive'.)

You need to be careful when dealing with costs. Although costs may be below forecast and therefore a minus, the effect upon the business will be positive, as costs are lower. It will nevertheless be necessary to analyse why the actual figure is lower than the forecast.

Budget and variance analysis

Just because the sales figure has a positive variance, this does not necessarily mean the business has done well. The positive variance could be due to:

- an improvement in the overall economy
- a change in the exchange rate
- a fall in tax (e.g. VAT being reduced from 17.5% to 15%)
- a fall in interest rates
- increased revenue due to an increase in inflation
- a change in the amount of competition
- a natural disaster
- a change in the quality of the raw materials
- how well motivated the employees are

Nevertheless, looking at individual parts of a budget, month by month or year on year, may help the business to focus on where the business is doing well and not so well.

Analysis

Analysis is likely to focus on variances, with reference either to their implications for the business, or to the reasons for them. Expressing your views clearly about the reasons for the variances will require you to develop your answer by offering step-by-step implications. It is not a good approach just to state, for example, that the variance was due to a change in the economic climate, which caused sales to fall. This will not gain a Level 3 mark. What is required is for you to show exactly how a change in the economic climate led to the variance.

- Recession led to higher unemployment.
- Higher unemployment meant that many consumers had less income.
- The products of the business are not necessities and therefore consumers cut back on purchases from the company, so its sales fell.

It is also acceptable to show calculations of the variance and then comment on the implications. (The calculation will be Level 2.)

Evaluation

There may be opportunities for you to suggest which reason for the variance was the most important, as long as you justify your choice.

Alternatively, evaluative comments may concentrate on the most likely implications for the business of a particular variance.

> **Examiner tip**
>
> It is important to note carefully whether the variance is positive or negative. Increases in revenue are positive and increases in costs are negative.

Cash flow

For many businesses, having sufficient cash to keep the business working (**working capital**) is one of the hardest issues to deal with. Cash flow is not about profit; it is about having enough cash within the business to pay the next set of costs.

Within a business plan and as part of an ongoing process, a business will prepare a **cash-flow forecast**. This is a prediction of the inflows (revenues) and outflows (costs) of a business.

This forecast should then be compared with the **cash-flow statement** of the business. This is a record of what the actual inflows and outflows were.

Inflows and outflows

Cash inflows are the total income (revenue coming into the business). They include:
- sales revenue
- loans
- sale of assets

Cash outflows are the total costs of the business. They include:
- raw materials
- wages
- utilities
- rent or purchase of factory

Opening and closing balances

The **opening balance** is the cash a business starts with at the beginning of a given period. The amount may be from a loan, if this is the first cash-flow forecast, or may include the closing balance from the previous period of time in the case of a business that is already established.

The **closing balance** is the amount of cash a business has at the end of a given period, either a month or longer. The closing balance of one period of time will become the opening balance of the next period of time (see Table 1).

Table 1 Cash-flow statement for 2012 (£)

Item	January	February	March
Opening balance	5,000	(5,500)	(3,500)
Sales revenue	7,500	22,000	27,000
Total inflows	**12,500**	**16,500**	**23,500**
Materials	8,000	10,000	11,000
Wages	10,000	10,000	11,500
Total outflows	**18,000**	**20,000**	**22,500**
Net cash flow	(5,500)	(3,500)	1,000
Closing balance	(5,500)	(3,500)	1,000

It is important to note, when looking at a cash-flow statement such as Table 1:
- whether the figures are a forecast or a statement
- what the period of time or date is, as this may be important when it comes to analysing the figures
- the denomination of the figures — whether they are in thousands or millions, or at face value
- how a negative cash flow is shown — most use brackets but a minus sign can also be used

Examiner tip

It is always worthwhile commenting on the period of time and, if possible, comparing with previous figures in order to establish any trends or issues.

Analysis of the cash-flow statement

Noting the points listed above is vital if you are to offer effective analysis. It is not clear from the statement in Table 1 how long the business has been trading; nor do we know what type of business this is. Similarly, you would need to know what the business is selling before commenting on the sales revenue. For example, the increase shown could be due to seasonal changes or a change in the economic climate.

The cash-flow statement can be used to show banks what the state of the business is, and what its needs are. In Table 1, sales revenue is continuing to grow without a similar increase in costs and therefore the business has a better (positive) cash flow.

Sources of cash-flow problems

Cash-flow problems can be caused by:
- a poor economic climate reducing sales revenue
- seasonal demand for the product or service
- holding too much stock
- customers paying late
- offering credit too readily, or credit periods too long
- increased tax payments

How to improve cash flow

Cash flow can be improved by:
- increasing cash sales
- selling assets
- borrowing
- factoring
- just-in-time production (holding less stock)
- leaseback
- reducing credit periods

Knowledge check 12

State three possible causes of cash-flow problems.

Analysis

Analysis can be shown when commenting on the consequences for the business if it has cash-flow problems. When there is a recession, the ability of consumers to buy goods is reduced and therefore sales revenue for the business will fall (reduced cash inflows). However, fixed costs (outflows) still have to be paid and therefore it is more likely that the business will suffer from a net cash outflow.

Similarly, analysis marks can be achieved by commenting on how increasing sales or borrowing will help improve the cash flow of a business.

Evaluation

Suggesting which method will improve the cash flow most effectively will ensure that Level 4 marks are gained.

Costs

Costs are important to all businesses. By keeping costs under control, it is easier to make a profit. Cutting costs can be an effective way of increasing profits without increasing sales. In a recession, it is often by cutting costs that profits are maintained.

Keeping costs under control is also essential in a competitive market.

Types of cost

Fixed costs

- Fixed costs (overheads or indirect costs) are not directly related to the level of sales (e.g. factory, machines, marketing, managerial salaries).
- They can increase in the long run as additional machines are purchased.
- They are drawn as a horizontal straight line (*FC* in Figure 4).

Variable costs

- Variable costs (direct costs) vary directly with the level of output (e.g. raw materials).
- They are often stated as a cost per unit of output.
- They are drawn as an upward-sloping straight line (*VC* in Figure 4).

Total costs

- Total costs are calculated as *FC* + *VC*.
- They are drawn as an upward-sloping straight line starting at the level of the fixed costs (*TC* in Figure 4).

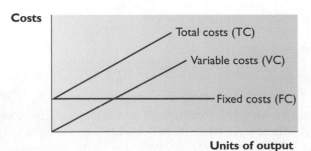

Figure 4 Fixed, variable and total cost curves

> **Examiner tip**
> Make sure you are familiar with the alternative names for the various types of costs.

Unit costs

- Unit costs are the cost of producing one good.
- They are calculated as: $\dfrac{\text{total costs}}{\text{output}}$
- Reducing unit costs increases the competitiveness of the business.
- Unit costs may fall as production increases (spreading the fixed costs).

Marginal costs

Marginal costs are the cost of producing one additional product.

Social costs

- Social costs are costs of production affecting others.
- When driving your car, the personal cost is the petrol you need to buy. The social costs are the pollution, noise and congestion caused by your journey.
- When consuming alcohol, the social costs may include the consequences of drinking to excess, criminal activities, pressure on health services, and increased noise, all of which affect the lives of others.
- These social costs are paid for not by the individual who bought the petrol or the alcohol, but by society as a whole.

Opportunity cost

- Opportunity cost is a way of considering the best option for a business when it spends money.
- It represents what the business could otherwise have spent the money on (what the alternatives were). For example, when a business buys a new machine, the opportunity costs might be a pay rise for the employees, or an additional marketing campaign.

Analysis

It is likely that analysis will be related to the consequences of changes in costs. Consequently, you will need to be comfortable with each type of cost to ensure that you offer the correct consequences. You will gain a Level 3 mark by showing that as production increases, the unit cost is likely to fall, and therefore the business may be able to reduce its prices in order to increase sales, or increase its profits. However, make sure you refer to the actual business to ensure a context. You may be able to comment on how the fall in unit costs will affect the ability of the business to achieve its objectives.

Evaluation

You could comment on the long-term and short-term effects of a fall in unit costs. Although in the short term costs will rise by purchasing a new machine, its running costs may be less and therefore in the long run the business's ability to compete may be increased, making the investment worthwhile. The new machine will probably be more productive and improve quality, so the business will be able to reduce its expenditure on replacing faulty goods.

Offering a justified judgement as to the overall effect on costs will gain a Level 4 mark.

Knowledge check 13

State the formula for calculating unit costs.

Knowledge check 14

Give two examples of social costs.

Contribution

Contribution or marginal costing

contribution per unit = price – variable (direct) costs

total contribution = sales × contribution per unit

profit = total contribution – fixed costs (overheads)

Example

Ice creams are sold for £1.50 each and the direct costs are 60p per unit. The overheads are £50,000. Sales of the ice creams are 75,000.

contribution per unit (price – direct costs) = £1.50 – 60p = 90p

total contribution (sales × contribution per unit) = 90p × 75,000 = £67,500

profit (total contribution – fixed costs) = £67,500 – £ 50,000 = £17,500

Special orders

It is important to ascertain whether it is worth taking on an additional order or special order. Contribution is a valuable tool in making such a decision.

If the order makes a contribution with or without an actual profit, it may well be worthwhile taking the order (as it is contributing to covering fixed costs).

In addition, the additional factors below might be considered before taking on a special order:
- Does the business incur any additional overheads from taking on the special order?
- Does the order make a positive contribution?
- Does it provide an opportunity for further additional orders?
- Does it help increase the number of consumers and therefore make the business less reliant on just a few?
- Does it have a detrimental effect on its existing customers?

Example

The normal price of an ice cream when sold to retailers is 50p. The direct costs are 20p. However, there is an opportunity for a special order to a new customer, a local chain of fast-food outlets that want to place an initial order for 2,000 ice creams but are only prepared to pay a price of 30p.

price of ice cream for new order = 30p

direct costs = 20p

contribution per unit (price – direct costs) = 10p

total contribution (contribution per unit × sales of 2,000) = £200

The contribution, although low, is positive and therefore the business may take the special order.

Examiner tip

Remember always to state the formula and show your working. Notice that the layout of this example is easy for the examiner to follow.

Knowledge check 15

State the formula for calculating contribution per unit.

Knowledge check 16

State the formula for calculating total contribution.

Knowledge check 17

If price = £15, direct costs are £4, sales are 35 and overheads are £250, calculate the profit.

Analysis

In the example above, the business may decide it is worthwhile taking this order, as it will provide an additional customer. Supplying a chain of fast-food outlets may lead to a large amount of future orders, reducing the need to rely on existing customers. It may also mean that the business will be able to increase its output and therefore reduce its unit costs (economies of scale), which in turn will help to increase its profits.

Evaluation

Making a justified judgement as to whether the business should take a special order will provide an obvious route to a Level 4 answer. Commenting upon the state of the existing business, its objectives, its existing resources and therefore its capacity to meet any additional orders, while ensuring that the additional order does not damage its relationships with existing customers, is an excellent way to achieve Level 4 marks.

Breakeven analysis

A business can use breakeven analysis to help in the decision-making process. Deciding how many goods need to be sold in order to cover costs, and what the profit or loss will be if a certain quantity of goods are sold, is always of value to a business.

Calculating breakeven

The formula for calculating the breakeven point for a product is:

$$\text{breakeven} = \frac{\text{fixed costs}}{\text{contribution per unit}}$$

Remember always to state the formula when calculating breakeven.

Example

A business produces ice cream and has fixed costs (overheads) of £20,000 and direct costs (variable costs) of 40p per unit. It hopes to sell each ice cream at £1.20.

To calculate the number of ice creams that need to be sold to break even:

$$\text{breakeven} = \frac{\text{fixed costs}}{\text{contribution per unit}}$$

$$= \frac{£20,000}{(\text{price} - \text{direct costs})} = \frac{£20,000}{120p - 40p} = \frac{£20,000}{0.8} = 25,000 \text{ ice creams}$$

Finding breakeven using a diagram

Breakeven can also be determined using a diagram. The breakeven point is where the total revenue is equal to the total costs (see Figure 5). To the left of the breakeven

> **Examiner tip**
> - Be careful when dividing pounds by pence.
> - Remember the answer for a breakeven calculation is a quantity, not a value.
> - Always show your working, stating the formula used.
> - If an answer is, for example, 277.4, it is always rounded up.
> - It is always of value to comment on your answer in terms of the ability of the business to achieve the breakeven level.

point, a loss is incurred as insufficient output is produced to cover all the costs. To the right of the breakeven point, a profit is made.

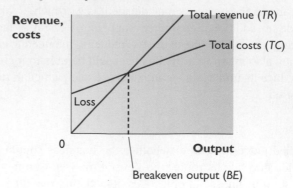

Figure 5 Breakeven output

Since revenue = price × output or sales, the gradient of the total revenue line will depend upon the price level. The higher the price, the steeper the gradient (see Figure 6). When price increases, the total revenue line becomes steeper (TR_2) and therefore the breakeven quantity falls (to BE_2).

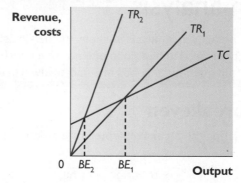

Figure 6 Effect of an increase in price on breakeven output

Figure 7 shows the effect of an increase in costs on the breakeven output. When the total cost line moves up (to TC_2), the quantity required to break even increases (to BE_2).

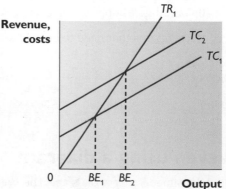

Figure 7 Effect of an increase in total costs on breakeven output

Margin of safety

The **margin of safety** is the difference between the actual level of output (1) and the breakeven output (2) in Figure 8.

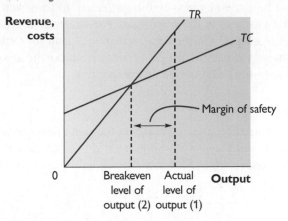

Figure 8 The margin of safety

Knowing the margin of safety is important to a business as it can assess the consequences of any changes in either revenue or costs. An increase in costs will increase the breakeven output and therefore reduce the margin of safety. A reduction in the margin of safety also leads to a fall in profits.

A large margin of safety provides a business with more scope to deal with changing circumstances that may affect sales.

Benefits of breakeven analysis

- The diagram gives a simplistic 'view' for interpretation.
- The calculation is quick to use.
- Breakeven aids the decision-making process.
- The level of profit or loss can be seen easily.
- The consequences of changes in revenue or costs can be found.
- The margin of safety can be shown.

Limitations of breakeven

- Changes in the level of fixed costs or variable costs make the calculation harder.
- Batch production makes the calculation harder.
- The assumption of one price is often unrealistic.
- Increases in price will not always increase total revenue, as sales may fall at the higher price.
- It assumes that output is sold.

Knowledge check 19

If actual production is 2,100 and breakeven level is 1,950, calculate the margin of safety.

Examiner tip
Ensure you are familiar with the benefits and limitations of breakeven as they are useful when assessing the value of this business tool.

Analysis

Many of the opportunities for analysis will come from either undertaking a calculation or drawing a diagram. Both will allow you then to comment on what will happen and how the business will be affected. In turn, you could go on to suggest how the business is likely to react. For example, if costs increase, the breakeven level of output will increase, which will lead to a smaller margin of safety. The business will receive less profit, which reduces the amount available to invest in the business in order to remain competitive.

Evaluation

Evaluative comments should concentrate on the most likely consequence for the business. However, you may want to comment on the limitations of the concept given the number of assumptions that are made, in the context of the business in the case study.

Investment appraisal

Investment appraisal is a decision-making tool that is used to assess whether an investment is worthwhile and feasible. There are two methods of investment appraisal that you need to know:
- payback
- accounting rate of return (annual average rate of return)

Payback

The payback method is used to assess how quickly an investment can be paid back. The quicker the payback, the lower the risk involved.

Calculating the payback period

Table 2 shows the cash inflows from an investment of £80,000. The table uses the following terms:
- EOY: end of year
- net cash inflow: revenue – direct costs
- cumulative cash inflow: taking account of inflows for each year
- payback period: the actual time taken to payback the investment

Brackets indicate a negative value.

Table 2 Payback over an exact number of years

Year	Net cash inflow	Cumulative cash inflow
EOY 0	0	(80,000)
EOY 1	20,000	(60,000)
EOY 2	30,000	(30,000)
EOY 3	30,000	0

Knowledge check 20

Which method of investment appraisal measures the degree of risk?

Examiner tip

It is important to show your workings clearly because you may still gain marks for these even if your final answer is incorrect.

The table shows that the payback period for this investment is 3 years. Notice that the clear layout shows exactly how payback has been calculated. You may need a similar layout to show the examiner what you have done.

In some calculations, the payback may not be an exact number of years. Table 3 shows the cash inflows from an investment of £90,000.

Table 3 Payback over an inexact number of years

Year	Net cash inflow	Cumulative cash flow
EOY 0	0	(90,000)
EOY 1	25,000	(65,000)
EOY 2	35,000	(30,000)
EOY 3	40,000	

In this case, payback takes place in the third year. To calculate exactly when:
- Take the amount still to be paid back at EOY 2: £30,000.
- Divide this amount by the net cash inflow of the next year: £40,000.

$$\frac{30,000}{40,000} = \frac{3}{4}$$

Therefore the payback period is 2 years and 9 months $\left(\frac{3}{4}\right)$ of a year.

Benefits of payback

- It is easy to use and interpret.
- It measures risk.

Limitations of payback

- It does not consider the value of money over time.
- It does not take account of any cash inflows after the payback period.
- It does not measure profitability.
- It does not show exactly when cash inflows occur.

Accounting rate of return

The accounting rate of return (annual average rate of return) measures the profitability of an investment.

Calculating the accounting rate of return

A business selling flags for sporting occasions wants to invest in a machine to produce the flags. The machine costs £50,000 and has a life of about 5 years.

The machine will generate cash flows for the 5 years as follows: £10,000, £15,000, £20,000, £20,000 and £15,000.

The accounting rate of return (ARR) is calculated as follows:
- Add the cash flows for each year:
  £10,000 + £15,000 + £20,000 + £20,000 + £15,000 = £80,000

Examiner tip

It is important to comment on your answer in the context of the actual business in order to decide if the payback period is acceptable.

Knowledge check 21

State two limitations of payback.

Examiner tip

It is useful to be able to comment on the limitations of an investment appraisal technique as this could be used as part of an evaluative statement as to the viability of a proposed investment.

- Subtract the cost of the investment:
  profit = £80,000 − £50,000 = £30,000

- Divide the profit by the life of the investment (5 years):
  annual average profit = $\dfrac{£30,000}{5}$ = £6,000

- Divide the annual average profit by the initial cost of the investment:
  annual average rate of return = $\dfrac{£6,000}{£50,000}$ × 100 = 12%

This information can then be used to assess whether the investment in question should be made.

Benefits of ARR

Knowledge check 22

State two benefits of using ARR.

- It counts all cash flows for the life of the investment (unlike payback).
- It measures profitability.

Limitations of ARR

- It assumes that forecasts of cash inflows are accurate.
- It does not consider the value of money over time.
- It does not indicate when cash inflows occur.
- The life of the investment may not be known.

Analysis

Doing these calculations is an obvious route into analysis, allowing you to comment on the significance of a percentage ARR or payback period. Suggesting whether an investment is worthwhile is analysis.

Evaluation

Evaluative answers will probably compare possible investments, suggesting which is the best. Remember to indicate that it is not only the length of the payback or the profitability of the investment that matters. It is important to offer a judgement in the context of the business. Can it afford to invest this amount of money regardless of the return or the payback? Which is more important to the business in the question, a short payback or a high rate of return?

Profit and loss

The profit and loss account

Knowledge check 23

State what is meant by the term trading period.

A **profit and loss (P&L) account** measures the level of profit or loss in a given period of time, usually 1 year. This period of time is known as a **trading period**.

Profit is calculated by subtracting the costs of the business from its revenue gained:

profit = total revenue (*TR*) − total costs (*TC*)

Table 4 shows a sample profit and loss account. The table uses the following terms:

- cost of sales = opening stock + stock bought – closing stock

- gross profit = sales revenue – cost of sales

- operating profit = gross profit – fixed costs (expenses)

- net profit = operating profit – interest paid

- retained profit = net profit – tax and dividends

Table 4 Profit and loss account: year ending 2012 (£)

(a) Sales revenue		250,000	
(b) Cost of sales	75,000		
(c) Gross profit		175,000	(a) – (b)
(d) Expenses	80,000		
(e) Operating profit		95,000	(c) – (d)
(f) Interest payable	10,000		
(g) Net profit		85,000	(e) – (f)
(h) Tax and dividends	25,000		
(i) Retained profit		60,000	(g) – (h)

It is important to note the following:
- Although the terms may vary, a clear layout is essential.
- The date of the accounts is important, as this may affect any analysis.
- Are the figures denominated in pounds, or thousands or millions of pounds?

Interpretation of the P&L account

In exam questions, you may be given figures for 2 years. This will enable you to make a comparison between the 2 years.

If an increased level of profit has been recorded, the P&L account will show whether this is due to growing sales revenue or costs falling.

Similarly, by comparing gross profit and operating profit, it is possible to see which costs (direct or indirect) have changed.

Benefits of using a P&L account

- It aids the decision-making process.
- It can be used to monitor progress and make comparisons with previous years.
- Stakeholders can use it as a source of information.
- Investors can use it to help them decide whether to invest in the business.
- HM Revenue and Customs requires it to ensure that the correct amount of tax has been paid.
- It is a legal requirement under the Companies Act for some businesses.
- The profit shown in the account is a valuable source of finance for the business.

Examiner tip
It is likely that at AS the examiners will ask you how useful accounts are to various stakeholders. However, it is still important to know the components of such accounts.

Knowledge check 24
Name two stakeholders that may benefit from seeing the P&L accounts of a business.

Analysis

Analysis is likely to focus on the value of such accounts. The P&L account provides essential information about the success or failure of a business. A healthy profit means that a bank will be more willing to lend money to the business and this will enable the business to expand and meet its objectives. Alternatively, the business will not need to borrow as much money, as the profit can be used as a source of finance. This will reduce the cost of borrowing, and help the business to keep its costs down and be more competitive.

Any comments about how the P&L account will affect the business or how the business is likely to react as a result of the P&L figures are valid routes to Level 3.

Evaluation

Indicating which benefit is the most important or which stakeholder will be most affected (positively or negatively) is the obvious way to gain Level 4 marks. It may be that a particular stakeholder will really benefit as a result of the figures given. Providing that you make it quite clear why a particular stakeholder will benefit (or lose) in the context of the case and the question, Level 4 marks should be obtained.

Balance sheets

A **balance sheet** is a statement about the value (or wealth) of a business at a given point in time. (This is different from a P&L account, which represents a period of time.)

Parts of the balance sheet

It is important that you know the contents of a balance sheet, although you will not be asked to undertake any detailed calculations. The balance sheet uses the following terms:
- **assets:** what the business owns
- **liabilities:** what the business owes
- **fixed assets:** the buildings/factory and equipment/machines required to produce the finished goods (also known as **tangible assets**)
- **depreciation:** an allowance for the wear and tear of machines. The longer the machines are used, the higher the depreciation (their value falls). Depreciation is subtracted to gain a more realistic value for fixed assets.
- **current assets:** assets that are not fixed within the accounting period, such as debtors, stock and cash
- **debtors:** money that is owed to the business
- **stock:** raw materials, work-in-progress and finished goods
- **cash:** money within the business
- **current liabilities:** money that is owed by the business to others
- **overdraft:** a short-term loan for less than 1 year
- **net current assets:** current assets – current liabilities
- **long-term liabilities:** loans for more than 1 year
- **net assets:** net current assets + fixed assets – long-term liabilities
- **capital employed (or shareholders' funds):** the value of funds tied up in the business's shares and retained profits

Knowledge check 25

State the three components of current assets.

Knowledge check 26

Net current assets = ?

The net assets and the capital employed should balance, as shown in the sample balance sheet in Table 5.

Table 5 Balance sheet: April 2012 (£)

Fixed assets	200,000		
Less depreciation 10%	20,000		
		180,000	
Current assets			
Debtors	15,000		
Stock	60,000		
Cash	5,000		
Total current assets		80,000	debtors + stock + cash
Current liabilities			
Overdraft	4,000		
Total current liabilities		4,000	
Net current assets		76,000	current assets – current liabilities
Long-term liabilities	90,000		
Net assets		166,000	fixed assets + net current assets – long-term liabilities
Shareholders' funds			
Ordinary shares	120,000		
Retained profit	46,000		
		166,000	

It is important to note:
- the date of the balance sheet
- the denomination of the figures, in pounds, or thousands or millions of pounds

Benefits of having a balance sheet

- It gives a value of the business at a moment in time.
- It is helpful to a bank when deciding whether to provide finance to the business.
- It is a measure of performance.
- It is useful to the business as it can see if it has sufficient funds to operate.
- Suppliers may want to see if the business can afford to pay.

Analysis

Analysis may be shown in considering the value of having a balance sheet. It enables a business to measure its performance for a given year and in comparison with previous years. This enables the business to take appropriate action if targets have not been met. Similarly, with a balance sheet the business is more likely to convince a bank to lend it money, assuming the balance sheet is healthy. This will enable the business to purchase the new equipment that will help it to remain competitive.

Examiner tip

It is important you are familiar with the components of the balance sheet and understand whether items are assets or liabilities. Noting the information in the balance sheet may help you know more about the 'health' of a business.

Knowledge check 27

Name two stakeholders that may be interested in the balance sheet of a business.

Evaluation

It may be applicable to offer a justified judgement as to which piece of financial information (P&L account or balance sheet) is more useful in the context of the business in the case study and the question given.

Summary

- Budgets are a forecast of future income and expenditure.
- Variance is the difference between the forecast and actual figures.
- Budgets are vital in managing the financial aspects of a business.
- Cash flow is important to ensure a business has sufficient finance to keep it working.
- Inflows are from revenue, loans and sale of assets.
- Outflows are from paying for utilities, raw materials, and wages.
- Cash-flow problems can be caused by a poor economic climate, poor sales and high costs.
- Total costs = fixed costs + variable costs.
- Marginal costs are the cost of producing one extra product.
- Opportunity costs represent the next best alternative that could have been bought.
- Contribution per unit = price − direct costs.
- Total contribution = contribution per unit × sales
- Total contribution − overheads = profit.
- Breakeven is calculated by dividing fixed costs by contribution per unit.
- Margin of safety is the difference between the actual level of output and the breakeven level (actual level − breakeven level).
- Two main methods of investment appraisal are payback and ARR.
- Payback measures the time it takes to cover the cost of investment and assesses risk.
- ARR measures the profitability of an investment.
- A P&L account measures the level of profits or losses within a period of time, usually 1 year.
- Gross profit = sales revenue − cost of sales.
- Operating profit = gross profit − fixed costs.
- Retained profit = net profit − tax and dividends.
- Balance sheets show the value of a business at a given point in time.
- Assets are what a business owns.
- Liabilities are what a business owes.
- Current liabilities refer to items of less than 1 year duration.
- Long-term liabilities are for more than 1 year.
- Stakeholders such as banks, shareholders, suppliers and employees are interested in P&L accounts and balance sheets.

People in organisations

Labour turnover

Labour turnover refers to the number of employees leaving a business in a particular period of time (usually in a year).

Calculating labour turnover

The formula is:

$$\text{labour turnover} = \frac{\text{number of employees leaving a business in a given time period}}{\text{average number employed in a given time period}} \times 100$$

Example

A business has 120 employees and 25 leave in the first year.

$$\text{labour turnover} = \frac{\text{number of employees leaving}}{\text{number of employees}} = \frac{25}{120} \times 100 = 20.8\%$$

Factors causing a high labour turnover

High labour turnover may be caused by:
- type of business — seasonal businesses will have a higher labour turnover
- difficult or unsociable working conditions
- a lack of motivation
- poor leadership or no recognition
- poor recruitment
- a boom economy, so there is plenty of employment choice for employees
- having young employees with no family ties
- poor training

Problems of high labour turnover

- With a high labour turnover, the costs of recruiting more employees will add to the total costs of the business.
- Staff will be diverted from productive tasks within the business and instead have to spend time selecting more employees. In a small business this is very time-consuming and expensive.
- New employees will require training — a further expense for the business.
- There will be more pressure on the experienced staff to produce the products and look after the new employees.
- If experienced or highly qualified staff leave, they will be harder to replace, especially in times when labour is in short supply.

Improving labour turnover

Methods of reducing a high labour turnover include:
- recruiting the right employees
- offering effective training
- offering sufficient motivation to encourage staff to stay
- offering a pleasant working environment (hygiene factor)
- providing opportunities for promotion (responsibility)
- rewarding long service
- offering opportunities for **job enrichment**

It is important to realise that for some businesses, a high labour turnover is almost inevitable.
- Seasonal work in agriculture and tourism is undertaken by people who will move around and not want to stay in one job for a long period of time.
- Students only require work for relatively short periods of time.
- The changing economy may well mean that employees have to be more flexible. They will change jobs more frequently to reflect the needs of an ever-changing business environment.

Examiner tip
Always state the formula for labour turnover and show your working. This is very important because if you make a mistake in your calculation, you will still gain some of the marks for knowledge.

Knowledge check 28

How is labour turnover related to employee motivation?

Job enrichment This makes the tasks an employee performs more varied and interesting and may also involve taking on more responsibility. Enrichment improves motivation and so can help lower labour turnover.

Knowledge check 29

State two *benefits* labour turnover might bring to a business.

Analysis

Indicating the consequences of a high labour turnover for the business in the case study will gain a Level 3 mark, as will comments on how the business might or should react to the problem.

Evaluation

Making comments about which factor affects labour turnover most for the business in the case is an obvious route into Level 4. Suggesting the most likely significant problems that the business in the case will face as a result of a high labour turnover will be equally effective. Finally, offering a judgement as to what is the best way to deal with the problem of high labour turnover, in the context of the case, will also be effective in gaining a Level 4 mark.

Theories of motivation

Motivation is a series of 'internal forces which spur us on to satisfy some need' (Child 1973). If employees are motivated, they are more likely to be productive, have less time off work and remain with the business, thereby reducing labour turnover.

Highly-motivated employees are essential if a business is to have a loyal, committed and efficient workforce.

Table 6 shows the main theories of motivation and their key features.

Table 6 Theories of motivation

Name of theorist	Theory	Key points
Taylor	Scientific management	• Pay by performance • Tight control of employees, organised like machines
Maslow	Hierarchy of needs	• Physiological, security, social, status, self-actualisation
Mayo	Human relations management	• Recognition • Sense of involvement
Herzberg	Two-factor theory	• Motivators: sense of achievement, recognition, responsibility, promotion, meaningful tasks • Hygiene factors: working conditions, pay, bureaucracy, status, job security
Drucker	Practice of management	• Setting targets • Pay • Promotion • Effective communication management • Sense of involvement
Peters	Thriving on chaos	• Recognition of good practice or skills • Involving employees • Financial incentives • Offering continuous employment

A worthwhile strategy to adopt is to discuss the similarities and differences between the motivational theorists. No marks will be awarded just for drawing Maslow's hierarchy of needs. It is much more effective to use the hierarchy to show how needs change and therefore to indicate that ways of motivating employees will also change.

You can use the theories listed in the table to help you justify a point that you want to make. Quoting a theorist can support your suggestions for how to motivate employees.

Analysis

An acceptable approach to gaining Level 3 marks is to make a point about how employees will be affected, positively or negatively, and to use the name of a theorist to support your point.

Evaluation

Making a justified judgement about which factor is the most likely to motivate employees in the context of the case, or stating which theorist is the most appropriate for a particular set of circumstances, will lead to a Level 4 mark. It is also possible to suggest that one approach or theorist's ideas will work better in the long run, even though it may be more expensive to implement than another theorist's ideas.

Methods of motivation

Personnel performance indicators

What is required to motivate the workforce will depend upon how content or happy employees are. The level of contentment can be measured using **personnel performance indicators**. These include:

- **Productivity of the employees.** The more productive they are, the more content. Actual productivity can be measured by taking the total output of the business and dividing it by the number of employees.
- **Absenteeism.** Absence without real reason (casual absenteeism) is calculated by taking the number of absences and dividing by the number of employees. High absenteeism is often a sign of a demotivated workforce.
- **Labour turnover.** This is the number of staff leaving in a given period of time, divided by the number of employees. High absenteeism may be the first sign that all is not well, but if problems are left unresolved, employees will leave.

Motivation methods

In order to motivate employees, there are several methods available.

Job enrichment

Making a job more interesting and varied is typical of job enrichment. According to Herzberg, giving more responsibility and a greater degree of involvement are motivators.

> **Examiner tip**
> High marks are not gained simply by producing a list of the motivational theorists and stating the nature of their work. Make sure you carefully select and *apply* the one(s) most likely to be relevant to the firm you are considering.

> **Knowledge check 30**
> What are the likely effects of a poorly motivated workforce?

> **Knowledge check 31**
> Why does a business use personnel performance indicators?

> **Job enrichment** This should involve redesigning and extending the sorts of tasks an employee performs, e.g. taking control of a whole task rather than just doing part of it. It will *not* improve motivation if employees are simply given more of the same sort of work.

Job rotation

If the tasks to be undertaken are rotated, even if there is no additional responsibility involved, employees experience greater variety.

Cell production

Unlike job rotation, cell production not only involves a variation in tasks to be undertaken but also has the additional element of greater responsibility for employees. Working in cells (teams), each member of the cell is responsible for the quality of the work undertaken. How the tasks are undertaken and by whom depends on the team members.

Teamworking

Charles Handy's term 'teamworking' refers to groups of employees who have a range of skills and are allowed to consider ways of constantly improving the productive process with which they are involved (**kaizen**). Companies that use teamworking, such as McDonald's, suggest that it has a positive effect upon the personal performance indicators.

Empowerment

Rosabeth Moss Kanter suggests that empowerment allows employees not only to undertake a range of tasks but also to take responsibility for how the task is performed and when it is undertaken. She considers that employees are in a better position to make such judgements, as they are the ones who actually perform the tasks.

Performance-related pay and incentive schemes

Although many theorists suggest that pay is not a motivator, it *is* of concern to employees. There are a wide range of performance-related pay schemes:

- piece rates: pay related to the level of output
- commission: pay related to the level of sales achieved
- bonuses: payments again related to achievement, however measured
- profit sharing: additional pay related to the level of profit
- shares: employees rewarded with shares
- benefits (perks): pensions, cars, healthcare, subsidised meals

These are all ways in which employers attempt to offer employees additional pay for good performance. However, it can be difficult to measure performance (especially for service industries) where there is no obvious 'output' to measure. For some, once such incentives have been awarded, they become an expected part of the employee's pay and therefore may lose the effect for which they were originally introduced. They may also cause envy among employees.

Analysis

There are several ways in which a Level 3 mark can be gained. Suggesting the likely implications for either the employees or the business of implementing a particular scheme is an obvious approach. However, it is also possible to indicate how the personnel performance indicators will be affected.

Performance-related pay This links pay in some way to performance and effort. If the correct method is chosen it can improve employee motivation.

Knowledge check 32

Outline three factors that should be considered if a performance-related pay system is to be successful.

Evaluation

Offering a justified judgement about which scheme will be the most appropriate, quickest to work, or cheapest to implement, will gain a Level 4 mark. Remember to use the context of the case.

Leadership

Leadership relates to the role of setting objectives for the business and ensuring that the business is a success. How the leader relates to and communicates with the workforce is significant, as it will affect how employees respond.

Leadership styles

Several different styles of leadership have been identified. These are summarised below with their key features.

Autocratic leadership

- This is characterised by a Tayloristic approach and coincides with McGregor's Theory X leadership (see p. 42).
- Decision making is quick, with little consultation.
- Tasks are set by the leader.
- The emphasis is on one-way communication.
- Tasks are supervised.
- There is little employee initiative.
- There is little evidence of the leader on the factory floor.

Democratic leadership

- This relates to Herzberg's motivators and coincides with McGregor's Theory Y leadership (see p. 42).
- Work-related issues are discussed.
- Decision making involves consultation and is therefore slower.
- Tasks are agreed with employees.
- Communication is usually two-way.
- There are opportunities for employee initiatives.
- The leader is often seen on the shop floor.
- Employees are involved.
- Employees take responsibility.

Laissez-faire leadership

- Employees set their own objectives.
- The leader is available if required.
- There are opportunities for employee initiatives.
- The decision-making process takes a long time.
- Employees are involved.

Leadership This is different to 'management' although the two are linked. A *manager* might be perfectly competent in terms of getting tasks completed but may do everything strictly 'by the book'. A *leader* on the other hand, will not only get the work done, but will be more inspirational and creative in his or her approach.

- Employees can have responsibility as the leader delegates almost all responsibility.
- Employees often lack a sense of direction.

Paternalistic leadership

- The leader makes the decisions.
- The leader encourages a sense of belonging towards employees.
- The leader encourages a sense of involvement in the business.

Other approaches to leadership style

McGregor's Theory X and Theory Y

Theory X and Theory Y are styles of leadership.

- **Theory X** leadership is characterised by an authoritarian approach by the leader. Like Taylor, the leader considers that employees do not like work and need constant control and direction.
- **Theory Y** leadership is characterised by a leader who encourages employees to use their initiative, and who attempts to maximise the commitment of employees.

Knowledge check 33

State three characteristics of a *poor* leader.

Tannenbaum and Schmidt's management grid

The different leadership styles lead to different approaches to decision making. These are shown on Tannenbaum and Schmidt's management grid in Figure 9.

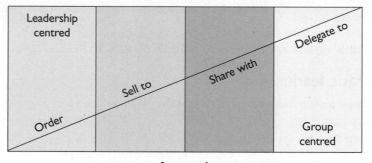

Approach

Figure 9 Tannenbaum and Schmidt's management grid

- **Leadership-centred management** means that employees are not involved in decision making and are less motivated.
- **Group-centred management** means that employees are involved in decision making and have responsibility. Therefore they are more motivated.

Management by objectives

Examiner tip

It is good practice to reinforce your comments about different styles of leadership and the consequences of those styles with a particular theorist's name.

According to Drucker's theory of management by objectives, once objectives have been agreed between employees and management, all involved will be aware of what is required and why. The objectives are trackable and have involved the employees.

Which leadership style should be used?

The leadership style to use depends on:
- the personality traits of the leader
- the skills of the leader
- the skills of the employees
- the tasks involved
- the size of the business
- the organisational structure of the business

Analysis

Highlighting the consequences of a particular leadership style for the business as a whole, or just for the employees, will gain Level 3 marks. Stating how a style will make it either easier or harder for the business in the case to achieve its objectives will also be worthy of Level 3 marks.

For example, if the leader uses a democratic style of leadership, the employees will feel a greater sense of involvement (Mayo) and are given more responsibility (Herzberg). This is likely to mean that the employees are motivated and therefore will be more productive, making it easier for the business to meet the deadline for delivery of a large order.

Evaluation

After discussing the various styles of leadership that could be used in the context of the case, selecting the most appropriate for the business in its particular set of circumstances, and justifying this choice, is a good route into a Level 4 answer.

Organisational structures

What is an organisational structure?

An organisational structure shows the way in which the business is organised. In visual form, it is a clear and concise method of indicating:
- who does what
- who is responsible for whom
- how many employees a person is responsible for
- the amount of delegation
- the span of control within the business

Types of organisational structure

Several different organisational structures and their main features are described on the next pages.

Organisational structure A business can be structured in one of several different ways, depending on its objectives and its culture. The structure of an organisation will determine the way in which it operates and how employees are expected to carry out their duties.

Organistic structure

- This is a flat structure with a large span of control (see Figure 10).
- There are a small number of layers.
- Each manager is responsible for a large number of employees.
- It is characterised by a democratic style of leadership.
- Delegation is encouraged.

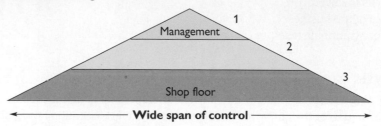

Figure 10 Organistic structure

Mechanistic structure

- This is a vertical structure with a small span of control (see Figure 11).
- Leadership is less democratic.
- There are a large number of layers.
- It is more bureaucratic.

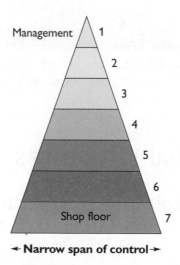

Figure 11 Mechanistic structure

Centralised structure

- In a centralised structure (see Figure 12), the style of leadership is likely to be autocratic.
- The leader is involved in all aspects of the business and there is little delegation.
- Everyone reports to the leader.
- Decisions are made at head office.
- Centralisation reduces the duplication of resources required to run the business.

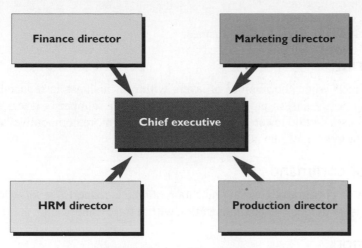

Figure 12 Centralised structure

Decentralised structure

- Decisions are made away from head office (more informed at a local level).
- The structure may be decentralised by area or product.
- There is a wider span of control.
- Leadership is more democratic.
- Employees are given responsibility (Herzberg).

Key concepts

Levels of hierarchy

The **levels of hierarchy** describe the number of layers within the structure. An organistic structure has few layers (flat), whereas a mechanistic structure has far more layers (vertical). The higher the number of layers, the harder communication becomes, as there are more layers for the message to pass through. However, the span of control (see below) tends to be smaller, so it is easier to control employees.

How many layers are in the hierarchy will depend upon:
- the size of the business
- the leadership style
- whether the business has a flat or vertical structure

Span of control

The **span of control** refers to the number of employees a manager is responsible for. The wider the span of control, the more employees the manager has to supervise. An ideal span of control is about 4 or 5.

There is a dilemma between a small span of control and a larger number of layers, which will hamper effective communication. The best span of control for a business will be determined by:
- the personality of the leader
- the employees' skills
- employees' willingness to take control of their own work

Knowledge check 34

Outline one advantage and one disadvantage of each type of organisational structure.

Examiner tip

Whether it is better for a manager to have a small or a large span of control is a good example of a business issue where there is no right answer. You must use the context of the case to make a judgement about the appropriateness of the business's span of control and the number of layers it has.

Rationalisation When a business rationalises it cuts costs — this usually involves reducing staffing levels. One way to rationalise is to reduce the number of levels in the hierarchy. However, the work that used to be performed by the employees who have been made redundant does not disappear; it will have to be moved up or down the new hierarchy. Therefore delayering means that there are implications for job enrichment and job enlargement.

Knowledge check 35

State the difference between 'span of control' and 'levels of hierarchy'.

- the size of the business
- the significance of costs to the business

Delayering

Delayering is when the number of layers within a business is reduced, often as part of a rationalisation programme. By reducing the number of layers within the business, costs can be lowered, making the business more competitive. With fewer layers, employees may gain additional responsibilities.

Chain of command

The **chain of command** gives an indication of who is responsible for whom. It also helps to assess the lines of communication within the business.

Delegation

Delegation is when responsibility is passed to employees. The more responsibility is given to the employees, the wider the span of control. The level of delegation will depend upon:
- the style of leadership
- the ability of employees
- what is to be delegated in terms of tasks or responsibilities

Empowerment

Empowerment is when employees are given responsibility for what they do within the business. It is a form of delegation and is a good way to motivate the employees (Herzberg and Mayo).

With empowerment comes the opportunity to delayer the business and therefore reduce costs.

Analysis

Be able to highlight the likely implications of adopting a particular organisational structure, with reference to the consequences for the span of control, the amount of likely delegation and the ability of the business to undertake effective communication.

Similarly, offer suggestions as to how delayering will affect the business.

The key concepts in this section can all be used to offer your thoughts on the possible consequences when there is a change in the management or organisational structure of the business in the case study.

Evaluation

Be able to offer a justified judgement as to which type of organisational structure would best suit the business in the case study, within the context of the question.

Comparing the positives and negatives of different structures, using concepts such as span of control, communication, delegation and chain of command, will enable you to gain Level 4 marks.

- Employees are a key resource in any business.
- Motivation is concerned with the forces that drive an employee to work hard. Motivation is vital to a business because motivated employees will be more productive and committed.
- One way of measuring motivation levels is to calculate the labour turnover figure for the firm as a whole and also for each department within it. High levels of labour turnover raise a firm's costs through expenditure on recruitment, selection and training.
- Motivation can also be measured through performance indicators such as absenteeism and labour productivity.
- There are many theories about the exact sources of employee motivation but there is no 'tick list' of policies that can be applied to every business to guarantee that it occurs. Nevertheless, certain broad principles can be identified (such as job enrichment, empowerment, and teamworking) which are likely to help bring it about.
- Although pay may not be the main motivator for all types of employee, it cannot be ignored. Modern payment systems recognise this and often incorporate some element of performance-related pay such as a bonus or profit sharing.
- The style of leadership adopted by a manager can affect employee motivation. There is no one correct style and good leaders will vary their style according to factors such as the business's situation, the nature of the task, and the employees' ability.
- There are different ways in which a business can be structured. The organisational structure of a business has implications for the likely leadership style and the role of its employees.
- Issues such as the length of the chain of command and management attitudes to delegation and empowerment in a business can have a major impact on human resource issues such as communication, coordination and motivation.

Operations management

The scale of operation

Why do businesses grow?

Businesses grow:
- to achieve greater profits
- to increase market share
- to improve their chances of survival
- to reduce costs

Types of growth

Internal (organic) growth is where a firm increases in size gradually over a period of time. A number of large businesses started off as small organisations.

External growth is where the business grows quickly, usually as a result of a takeover or merger. This sort of growth requires a ready source of finance.

Capacity

Capacity is the maximum amount of output that the business can produce given its current resources. These resources are buildings, machinery and labour.

Takeover A company or person buys 51% of the shares in another company and can then legally outvote all the other shareholders. Takeovers are often hostile. The directors of the company under threat might recommend to existing shareholders that they reject the offer being made to tempt them to sell.

Merger Two firms join together to create a new business, although the existing brand names may survive, e.g. the Orange and T-Mobile merger in 2010. A merger usually occurs on an agreed basis.

Capacity utilisation is the percentage of the available capital that the firm is using at one time. If a business is producing 90,000 units when its capacity is 100,000, its capacity utilisation is 90%.

Capacity utilisation is important. A firm does not want expensive fixed assets lying idle. If machinery is not producing it is not generating products for sale.

Capacity utilisation is often used as a measure of efficiency.

Under-utilisation of capacity

This may be a consequence of:
- a fall in demand
- seasonal variations
- an increase in the available capacity
- inefficiency in the production process

Under-utilisation of capacity can be an advantage because it reduces pressures on the business. However, it increases the fixed costs per unit and might result in price rises.

Over-utilisation of capacity

If capacity is being over-utilised, businesses can increase capacity in the short term by:
- increasing the hours each employee works per week
- moving workers between jobs
- subcontracting work to outside agencies

The problems with pushing capacity to the limit are that:
- Workers may become demotivated.
- The quality of the product may suffer.
- Sales could be lost.

Economies and diseconomies of scale

Internal economies of scale

Internal economies of scale are benefits that the business achieves as its size increases, which result in a lower cost per unit of output.
- **Purchasing economies.** These are gained through being able to buy raw materials in bulk.
- **Financial economies.** The larger the business, the more likely it is that it will be able to borrow and that it will be given preferential rates.
- **Managerial economies.** Large firms can employ specialist managers who are likely to make the firm more efficient.
- **Technical economies.** Larger firms can buy more specialist equipment, which will reduce the unit cost of production through efficiency gains.
- **Marketing economies.** Larger firms can afford more varied methods of promotion, and particularly above-the-line promotion.
- **Risk-bearing economies.** Large firms can diversify into new markets and products, and spread their risks.

Knowledge check 36

Outline two reasons why a growth in sales may not lead to an immediate rise in profit.

Knowledge check 37

How does a business calculate its capacity utilisation?

Examiner tip
Although growth is frequently one of a firm's medium- or long-term objectives, you should not assume that growth in sales automatically means a growth in profit. Many exam questions are set on why this is the case.

External economies of scale

External economies are achieved as a result of the whole industry growing. They usually arise because a number of similar firms are located together.

- **Concentration economies.** These economies may come through attracting specialist labour or because specialist supply firms locate in the vicinity.
- **Information economies.** Firms can benefit from the increase in information that passes between them.

Diseconomies of scale

These are disadvantages that arise as the firm grows in terms of increased costs per unit of production. They often occur when a business reaches a particular size.

- **Communication problems.** As firms grow, it becomes more difficult to communicate quickly and effectively.
- **Problems in managing the production process.** Large firms may find it increasingly difficult to organise the complexities of production.
- **Reduction in morale.** As communication problems arise, workers tend to feel less important. They may feel that their views are not important and that management is unaware of the problems they face. Labour turnover often rises as a result.

Analysis

Analysis should consider the consequences for the firm increasing in size in terms of its sales and profits. For example, if production increases, the unit costs will fall and therefore the business can either increase its profits or reduce its prices in order to capture a larger share of the market.

Evaluation

Evaluation marks can be achieved by discussing the best scale of operation for the business. This can be viewed in terms of profits, the wishes of the owner, the sector of the economy or the long-term prospects for profit.

Organising production

Should production be labour- or capital-intensive?

A firm that is labour-intensive will have a large number of processes that need to be done by hand. An example is the production of pottery character figures.

A firm that is capital-intensive will use machinery in most of its processes. An example is the production of mobile phones.

In recent history, many labour-intensive firms, such as the car industry, have become increasingly capital-intensive as machines, computers and robotic production have been introduced.

Examiner tip

Do not confuse *total cost* with *unit cost*. Total cost will always rise as a firm increases output as more employees are taken on and more raw materials purchased, but if it is able to gain economies of scale then the unit cost will fall.

Knowledge check 38

How are total costs and unit costs calculated?

Examiner tip

It is important to recognise that, in itself, it is not a communication problem or a reduction in morale that causes unit cost to rise. However, if production slows down (or falls) as a result of such factors, as total costs are still rising, output will no longer be growing at a sufficient rate to push down the unit costs and so they will rise.

Methods of production

- **Job production.** This involves completing a whole product before going on to the next unit of production (e.g. a musical instrument).
- **Batch production.** In this system a group of products are produced together as a batch (e.g. granary bread rolls in a bakery).
- **Flow production.** In this method, goods move through the process from one stage of production to another (e.g. televisions).
- **Cell production.** This involves the organisation of workers into groups or cells so that each cell makes a product from start to finish (e.g. slippers).

The method of production chosen has implications for the type of capital and labour that need to be used and also for the likely unit cost of the product.

Which is the best method?

The advantages and disadvantages of each method of production are listed below.

Job production

Advantages

- Consumers are willing to pay high prices for individual workmanship.
- Staff are better motivated.
- Quality is high.
- There is increased customer satisfaction.

Disadvantages

- It takes time to produce the product.
- As a consequence, production costs are higher.
- Little use is made of capital equipment.
- It often takes a long time to deliver the finished product to the customer.

Batch production

Advantages

- It is faster than job production.
- The costs are lower than with job production.
- There is a greater ability to meet demand quickly.

Disadvantages

- Worker motivation may be lower.
- There is more downtime because of stopping and starting new batches.
- The system requires higher stock levels.
- There is a loss of individuality and, possibly, quality.

Flow production

Advantages

- Costs per unit of output are low.
- There is no product variation.
- Levels of output are higher.

Disadvantages

- Production can be inflexible and unresponsive to demand.
- There is lower worker motivation.
- Breakdowns in the process cause problems further down the line.
- The start-up costs for capital equipment are high.
- Workers have less responsibility for the final product.

Cell production

Advantages

- There is more teamwork, which improves motivation.
- Quality is better because the team is accountable for the units produced.
- Workers can become multi-skilled and the work is more varied.
- Less stock is required.

Disadvantages

- The jobs require teamwork.
- Output may be lower than in flow production.
- The factory layout may need to be more complex.

Which method?

Choosing the right method depends on:

- **The type of product.** Individual orders will require different methods from producing identical output.
- **Demand for the product.** Designer items will face lower demand, but the requirement for quality and individual finish will be high.
- **Size of the firm.** Small firms will not have the space for cell production or be able to afford large amounts of capital equipment.
- **The availability of suitable capital equipment/technology**.

Analysis

Look at the implications for the business of using a particular type of production method. For example, the introduction of cell production might result in higher motivation and efficiency, reducing the cost per unit for the business and offering the potential to increase profit or sales.

Evaluation

Evaluation marks can be gained by coming to a conclusion about the best method of production for a particular business, having weighed up the options first.

Examiner tip

Students tend to assume that flow production is usually 'best' because it has the potential to considerably lower the firm's unit costs, but you must carefully weigh this advantage against its possible disadvantages.

Knowledge check 39

State the factors that might affect a business's choice of production method.

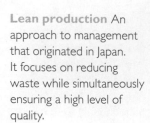

Lean production

What is lean production?

Lean production is a collection of techniques intended to minimise waste. It includes the following elements:
- continuous improvement or kaizen (see p. 57)
- cell production (see p. 50–51)
- just-in-time production (see p. 58)
- time-based management — this involves methods of production that reduce the time taken in getting the product to market

Advantages of lean production

The advantages of lean production are:
- increased motivation of workers
- higher quality of output
- an improvement in cash flow
- higher worker participation
- increased levels of output

Disadvantages of lean production

The disadvantages of lean production are:
- There is less opportunity to gain economies of scale because of small-scale orders of stock.
- All staff need to feel involved in the process.
- The firm may be unable to respond quickly to changes in demand.
- The system cannot work without a good supply chain.

Lean production versus mass production

Lean production and mass production are compared in Table 7.

Table 7 Mass production and lean production compared

Mass production	Lean production
High levels of stock	Reduced stock levels (just-in-time?)
Flow production (continuous)	Adaptable production (often cell and/or batch)
Quality inspection	Inbuilt defect prevention
Low skill level of workforce	Highly skilled workers
Large-scale deliveries	Small-scale deliveries
Higher economies of scale	Lower economies of scale

Examiner tip
Remember, a business does not simply introduce lean production. The process has a huge number of implications such as renegotiating contracts with suppliers and retraining employees. Such changes must be carefully planned and implemented — preferably with considerable employee involvement.

Analysis

Analysis marks can be achieved by discussing the benefits to the firm of adopting lean production. These will usually come from greater efficiency in production and lead to lower costs and higher profits.

Evaluation

Evaluation can be shown by explaining whether the business should choose to use lean production or mass production and also by explaining how the benefits arise for the firm.

Quality

What is quality?

Quality is defined as the ability to satisfy the consumer. Products are judged by consumers on the basis of ability to perform, durability, reliability, image, after-sales service and value for money.

It is very difficult to measure quality and for the business to control it. One way in which a business can try to do this is through value analysis.

Advantages of high quality

The advantages of producing high-quality goods are:
- It enables the firm to charge higher prices (e.g. Audi cars).
- It should reduce waste in the production process.
- The firm will not need to spend as much on advertising. Word-of-mouth will promote the product.
- Customer complaints should be reduced and there is less likelihood of legal disputes.
- Firms such as John Lewis that market high-quality goods are able to offer longer warranty periods. This increases demand, despite the fact that John Lewis's prices may not be particularly low.

Improving quality using quality circles

Quality circles are short meetings of workers in which problems associated with production and the maintenance of quality are discussed. They are held regularly and frequently to resolve problems as they arise. They prioritise issues and present solutions to management.

Advantages of quality circles
- Quality circles increase worker motivation.
- They improve communication between management and workers.
- They give workers the opportunity to show their expertise in the areas where they are working.
- Quality becomes an integral part of the production process.

Disadvantages of quality circles
- Time and money are taken up by the need for regular meetings.
- Some employees who are not involved may be resentful.
- The objectives of the workers and management involved may be very different in terms of outcomes.

State two characteristics of lean production.

Quality It is impossible to overstate the importance of quality in a competitive globalised market place. Some firms operate a total quality management system (TQM) that gives each employee responsibility for delivering quality. This can vastly reduce waste but it can take a long time before results are delivered; it should not be seen as a 'quick fix'.

Quality circles These result from a 'Theory Y' view of the workforce. Employees are seen as a valuable resource who can be encouraged to identify and solve work-related problems. If used properly, they can not only enrich the lives of employees but also bring benefits such as improved productivity and the reduction of waste.

State three factors a firm should take into account if it was considering the introduction of quality circles.

Analysis

Analysis marks can be achieved by discussing the effects of initiating quality circles in a firm. It will have benefits that might result in higher quality, more efficient production and better worker morale. All of these are likely to result in better performance by the firm and therefore increase sales revenue, which in turn may increase profit.

Evaluation

It is possible to show evaluation by weighing up the advantages and disadvantages of creating a system of quality circles. An alternative might be to compare the use of quality circles with another method of improving efficiency, such as kaizen, and then to decide which would be the more effective.

Stock control

Stock

Stock and its management are a major problem for many firms. Any business needs to have access to sufficient stock in order to produce efficiently. However, holding too much stock creates problems for the business, ties up working capital and incurs costs.

Stock can fall into one of three categories:
- raw materials
- work-in-progress
- finished goods

The cost of stock

Knowledge check 42

State three reasons why stock control is an important issue for a business.

The more stock that the business holds, the higher the costs it incurs. However, the firm cannot afford to run out of stock, as this will halt the production process.

In buying stock, the business needs to consider the storage facilities that are available. Bulk buying may reduce the cost per unit.

The firm must also ensure that its stock levels allow it flexibility when meeting demand.

Stock control charts

Stock control charts (see Figure 13) monitor the level of stock over a period of time. They plot:
- the **maximum level** of stock that the firm wants to hold
- the **minimum level** that the stock can be allowed to fall to (also known as the **buffer stock level**
- the **reorder level**, which is the point at which a new order for stock must be placed
- the **lead time**, which is the amount of time that will elapse between the order being placed and the stock being delivered

Examiner tip

Always read a stock control chart with great care, noting the denominations and time periods.

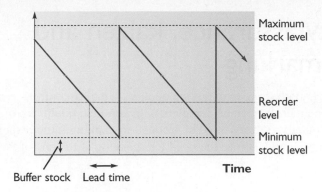

Figure 13 Stock control chart

Example

A firm has a maximum stock that can be stored of 2,700 units.

The firm uses 200 units per day. The lead time for delivery is 2 days. This means that the business must always have at least 400 units in stock.

To ensure that production can be guaranteed, even if there is a delay in deliveries, the firm sets its buffer stock level at 800 units. This will give 4 days' production.

New stock is reordered when the stock level falls to 800 units.

Managing stock usage

Overall stock efficiency can be managed by:
- **Stock rotation.** This needs to be used to prevent new stock being used before old stock. It is particularly important when stocks are perishable or degrade with time.
- **Computer-based stock control.** Many firms, particularly supermarkets, now handle stock control using computers. This is called **electronic point of sale (EPOS)**. Every sale going through the electronic tills will reduce the level of stock figures, making monitoring instant.
- **Reducing stock levels.** This is usually referred to as **just-in-time** production or stocking (see p. 58).

Analysis

Marks for analysis can be achieved by considering the method of stock control used by a firm. For example, the introduction of a system to keep stockholding to a minimum will lower the firm's costs and improve its cash-flow position. This will enable the business to remain competitive.

Evaluation

Different methods of stock control can be compared to see which will be best for a particular firm. For example, a business would need to compare the savings from just-in-time stock control with the need to ensure that there is always sufficient stock to guarantee production.

Examiner tip

If you are going to offer comments on what sort of stock control system a business should operate, make sure that what you recommend will ensure that (a) the firm has the right amount of stock in the right place at the right time, (b) excessive amounts of capital are not tied up unnecessarily, and (c) production will still be able to continue even if problems arise with suppliers.

Quality assurance, kaizen and benchmarking

The traditional approach to maintaining quality — quality control — was to produce the product and then check it on completion. In contrast, quality assurance methods try to ensure quality at every stage of production, making it the responsibility of all employees. This should remove the need for checking at the end of the process, and reduce waste.

Quality control

Quality control checks production by looking at examples of the finished product.

Advantages of quality control

- Those doing the checking are experts.
- Inconsistencies in pattern are easy to spot.
- Defective products can be picked out easily and removed.

Disadvantages of quality control

- It is a negative way of measuring the workers' performance.
- The workforce can be unconcerned about the quality of production because they know that faults will be picked up at the end.
- Not every product is checked.
- It is wasteful. Products that should be taken out of production in the early stages go through the whole system of production.
- It is expensive.

> **Examiner tip**
> If you are discussing productivity remember that it is output per worker, not total output.

Quality assurance

Quality assurance is a system for monitoring quality at every stage of production.

It is based on the customers' requirements for the product, using the notion of the 'internal customer'. Each process regards the next stage of production as its customer. This encourages workers to take care of the quality of what they produce.

'Total quality' removes the need to inspect products at the end of the process.

Advantages of quality assurance

- Workers take more care in production.
- There is increased motivation of workers as they are given responsibility for quality.
- Costs are reduced because checking is done at every stage.
- The workers are the best people to enforce quality in the production process.

Disadvantages of quality assurance

- The workforce may not be prepared to operate the system, particularly if payment is by output produced.

- The process places greater demands on workers.
- There are start-up costs in terms of training.
- In some product markets, quality may not be vitally important, so time will be wasted and costs may rise.

Total quality management (TQM)

According to Deming, **total quality management** is a 14-point plan for the operation of quality assurance. Its main features are:

- Get it right first time — prevent rather than detect later.
- All staff must accept the process.
- Constantly improve.
- Supervisors should encourage rather than find fault.
- Set achievable goals.
- Encourage workers to take pride in their work.
- Train and educate.

Kaizen

Kaizen means continuous improvement. The term comes from Japanese work processes. In this system, workers are involved in making improvements to the production process. The changes involved are often small.

Advantages of kaizen

- When it is first introduced, productivity (output per worker) improves.
- It eliminates waste.
- It lowers the firm's breakeven point.
- It makes the business more responsive to customer needs.
- It is simple to use and has low costs.
- It helps improve worker morale and safety.

Disadvantages of kaizen

- Some workers may not want to be involved in the process.
- It can be difficult to implement for a new workforce.
- The setting-up costs may be a problem.

Benchmarking

Benchmarking involves implementing the system that is 'best practice' in the industry. It means finding the best way of doing a particular task by looking at what others in the same industry are doing.

Advantages of benchmarking

- By observing others, a firm can find better ways to complete tasks.
- Targets can be set based on what is achieved elsewhere.
- Benchmarking reduces costs and waste.

Knowledge check 43

Give two advantages for a business of operating a policy of quality assurance.

Examiner tip

Quality assurance schemes, like kaizen, can be linked to motivational theory, e.g. a sense of involvement (Mayo) and having responsibility (Herzberg).

Examiner tip
Introducing methods
of quality assurance or
quality management are
good ways of improving
productivity (output per
worker) in a business.

Disadvantages of benchmarking

- It can be difficult to get accurate data.
- Copying rather than leading can become the norm for a business.
- The cost of collecting the information may be higher than the gains achieved.

Analysis

It is possible to use any of the quality control and assurance methods to discuss the benefits that the firm will achieve from implementation. For example, as a result of introducing TQM, a business should find that it produces better-quality products, which should increase consumer demand and lead to higher turnover.

Evaluation

Evaluation can be shown by discussing the costs and benefits of introducing a system of quality assurance. A decision could then be made about whether it would be worthwhile to continue with its introduction. Alternatively, evaluation marks could be achieved by justifying which would be the best method of quality assurance for the firm to pursue.

Just-in-time and waste management

Just-in-time

Just-in-time (JIT) production is a system where stockholding is reduced by not ordering stock or by not producing goods until they are required. By using this method, some firms are able to hold zero stock in any category.

- Components and raw materials are not ordered until required.
- Production is not begun until an order is received.
- The finished product leaves production and is delivered to the shop or direct to the customer.

Advantages of JIT

- It reduces stock levels.
- It avoids overproduction.
- Closer links are made with the customer.
- There is a reduction in waste.
- Quality improves because the product is made with the customer in mind.
- Costs are reduced.

Disadvantages of JIT

- It requires good communication.
- Supply problems may arise if suppliers are not reliable.
- Worker flexibility is essential.
- There may be a loss of economies of scale.

Examiner tip
JIT stock control is used
in the manufacturing and
retail sectors to remove the
disadvantages of holding
large amounts of stock.

Waste management

What is waste?

The term 'waste' refers to anything that is inefficient in production. It can invove any of the following:

- overproduction
- waiting for a delivery
- over-processing
- over- or under-stocking
- poor factory layout
- scrapping of defective or damaged products

Improving waste management

Waste management can be improved by:

- introducing just-in-time methods to stocks or production
- improving links with supplicrs
- organising the factory layout to improve efficiency
- coordinating production with marketing so that the consumers' demands are better matched
- improving quality control

Knowledge check 44

Give two benefits for a business of using a system of JIT stock control.

Analysis

Consider the benefits to the business of adopting just-in-time methods or managing waste more effectively. Such methods could result in a lower cost per unit or ensure that customer demands are being better met. Either would lead to an increase in profits and provide finance for the future.

Evaluation

Level 4 marks could be achieved by weighing up the costs and benefits of introducing just-in-time methods. A decision could be reached about whether it is a sensible path for the firm to follow.

Summary

- It is important for a business to utilise its capacity effectively. A low level of utilisation means that unit fixed costs are high. A high level of utilisation means that essential maintenance may not be possible and quality may suffer as a consequence.

- If a business is able to gain economies of scale its unit costs will fall. This is important because it means the profit per unit sold is increased.

- Diseconomies of scale usually arise from human factors that lower productivity. This fall in productivity causes unit costs to rise, thus lowering the profit per unit sold.

- Production can be capital or labour intensive depending on the nature of the product, e.g. consumer durables such as fridges will be produced in a capital intensive process whereas services such as healthcare will be labour intensive.

- There are four methods of production: job production, batch production, flow production and cell production. All have different implications for the business.

(Summary continues over the page)

Summary

(Continued)

- Lean production is a collection of techniques intended to minimise waste and simultaneously improve quality. It is desirable but is not something that should be introduced without very careful planning and extensive stakeholder consultation.

- 'Quality' means that a product (or service) is fit for purpose, i.e. it satisfies the consumer in terms of factors such as performance, image, reliability, and value for money. It is essential in a globalised competitive marketplace.

- 'Quality control' is not the same as 'quality assurance'. The latter is the more modern concept that quality is the responsibility of every employee at every stage of production rather than a quality control officer checking finished items.

- One way of improving production techniques is to use benchmarking, i.e. implementing the system that is 'best practice' in the industry. However, it needs to be recognised that it is one thing identifying a benchmark and quite another to implement it in a different firm.

- Stock control is an important issue for a business. A balance needs to be struck between holding sufficient stock (which involves a storage cost) and minimising it (which may involve an 'out of stock' cost in terms of lost customer orders).

- Just-in-time (JIT) production means not ordering stock or not producing goods until they are required. By using JIT, stocks can be minimised or even eliminated altogether.

- 'Waste' refers to anything that contributes to inefficiency in production. The reduction of waste is important because lower levels of waste mean lower unit costs.

Questions & Answers

This section comprises two case studies. Both have been written to reflect accurately the type of questions you will face in your examination for Unit F292. The format and the mark allocation mirror what you will be faced with in the unit examination.

It is strongly recommended that you attempt the questions before you read the examiner's comments and the student answers. This will encourage you to practise your exam technique and allow you to compare your answers with those provided.

Once you have attempted the case study questions, it is recommended that you look at the initial examiner's comments, which highlight the type of answer expected by the examiner (shown by the icon ⊜).

Following this are actual answers written by students. Included within these answers are letters **a**, **b** etc. which correspond to examiner's comments on each answer. These comments are intended to show you exactly what is rewarded and what is not. They also clearly highlight within the student answers where a particular level of response is achieved. Examiner's comments are preceded by the icon ⊜.

At the beginning of the examiner's comments, the mark awarded for the question is shown. A total mark is then shown, together with the grade awarded, at the end of each set of answers. All answers are A grades.

Levels of response

One of the key routes to success is understanding levels of response. Answering the questions using the appropriate level of response will mean that you are approaching the question in the right manner. Understanding how examiners use 'trigger words' will help you to identify which level of response is required.

Level of response	Definition
Level 1	**Knowledge** • Business knowledge or facts
Level 2	**Explanation or application** • An explanation or understanding of knowledge
Level 3	**Analysis** • Implications for the business • How the business is affected • The reaction of a business or stakeholder • All should be in the context of the case
Level 4	**Evaluation** • Making a justified judgement in the context of the case • Weighing the evidence/arguments, long term and short term in the context of the case • Suggesting which issue raised is the most significant, the most likely to affect the business or the most serious factor to affect the business

Mastering what is required for each level of response should be a high priority.

Ensuring that you are able to offer analysis and evaluation is essential if you are to achieve the top grades.

Analysis

Consider the example of Business A which is about to invest in new technology by buying a new machine. The following paragraphs show how easy it is to gain a Level 3 (L3) mark.

The owners of the business will be able to produce more items as the new machine is much more efficient. Therefore with more goods being produced, the business will be able to increase its revenue from the extra sales. This additional revenue will help the business to make more profit (L3) and therefore it will be able to offer a higher dividend to its shareholders (L3).

Being able to produce more goods with the new machine may, however, lead to a fall in the number of employees needed. The employees may therefore either lose their jobs or be fearful of losing their jobs, which may affect their productivity (L3).

With the new machine and the subsequent increase in output, the suppliers to the business will have the opportunity to sell more of its components and therefore increase its sales revenue. It may mean the supplier will need to take on more employees (L3), which will benefit the government, as it will have to pay out less in job seeker's allowance (L3).

Clearly stating the likely implications for the business or stakeholders, or how the business may react, in the context of the case, is a common and effective way in which to gain Level 3 marks.

Evaluation

Similarly, evaluative statements require you to make a justified judgement. The judgement can be related to the most likely effect, or the factor that will have the most beneficial or detrimental effect upon the business. The following paragraph shows you how to achieve Level 4 (L4) by using evaluation.

The stakeholder which will benefit the most is likely to be the shareholder. As a result of the increased output from the new machine, it is very likely that the increased sales will mean additional profits that could be distributed in the form of dividends to the shareholders. This is more certain than the possibility of redundancies as a result of the machine. It is not certain if the machine is used instead of employees. With the increased output the firm may actually require additional employees and not fewer (L4).

Here the student has made a judgement which suggests that one group of stakeholders will benefit more than another and has justified this view in the context of the case.

It is not enough just to begin your answer 'In evaluation…' — you have to make a judgement that has been justified in context.

Trigger words

Each question will have a key trigger word or phrase that should give you a clear indication of the appropriate level of response. These are listed in the following table. Levels of response are also referred to as assessment objectives (AOs).

Trigger words	Level of response	Assessment objective
State, list	Level 1	AO1
Explain, outline, describe	Level 2	AO2
Analyse	Level 3	AO3
Evaluate, assess, to what extent, discuss, recommend	Level 4	AO4

Mark allocation

	Mark allocation
4-mark question	• Level 2, 3–4 marks • Level 1, 1–2 marks
16-mark question	• Level 4, 12–16 marks • Level 3, 7–11 marks • Level 2, 3–6 marks • Level 1, 1–2 marks
20-mark question	• Level 4, 15–20 marks • Level 3, 9–14 marks • Level 2, 4–8 marks • Level 1, 1–3 marks

Examination format

It is important that you are aware of the examination format. Your teacher will no doubt have made this clear to you at an early stage in the course, but the format is summarised here.
- Length of examination: 2 hours
- The total marks for this paper represent 60% of the total AS marks.

This is a pre-issued case study paper, where the stimulus material is approximately three pages in length (though it will vary, depending upon the number and type of appendices).

There are two sections:
- Section A has one six-part question that requires short answers. These questions are *not* related to the pre-issued case.
- Section B has four questions based on the pre-issued case. The questions can come from any section of the specification. They will be a combination of short-answer, 'state'-type questions, 'analyse' questions and questions that will require you to evaluate.

You have to answer the questions in an answer booklet. This contains each question followed by a space for your answer.

Weightings for the different assessment objectives (levels of response) as a percentage of the total AS marks are shown in the table below.

	AO1 (L1)	AO2 (L2)	AO3 (L3)	AO4 (L4)	Total
Business Functions	15%	16%	15%	14%	60%

It is worth noting that the weighting for the levels of response differs from those in Unit F291, especially for Levels 3 and 4.

Case studies

As the examination papers you will take at AS and A2 are based on case studies, it is essential that you are able to use the context of the case. In order to do this, it is worthwhile adopting the 'first read' and 'second read' approach.

First read

Read the case quickly to ascertain:
- the type of business (its legal status — Ltd, plc, sole trader) or its age or size
- the product or service
- the consumers
- the objectives of the business

These four factors will provide you with a framework in which to answer the questions.

Second read

Read the questions and then read the case again. This is a more thorough read when you can start looking for information within the case to answer the questions posed. You will, of course, have plenty of time to study the case as it is pre-released.

For this module, the case material is approximately three pages in length and provides a context for you to use. For Level 3 and Level 4 answers, you are expected to use the context in order to gain the marks.

Case study 1 **Perry and Joseph Cottages**

2 hours

Perry and Joseph Cottages (P&J) was established in the 1990s with the purchase of two cottages in the Lake District, adjacent to Lake Windermere. Both were in serious need of repair, and Perry, a carpenter by trade, renovated them with the help of a group of contractors.

Since then Joseph, the brains behind the business, acquired more and more properties in and around the Lake District. Both thought that the demand for holiday cottages would continue to rise as incomes rose and people's leisure time also increased. Escaping for the weekend or for a longer break at any time of the year meant that business should be brisk and the profits subsequently high — high enough to allow Joseph to continue to buy properties for Perry to work on, getting them fit to let out to a wide range of customers.

P&J owned over 25 properties. This meant that as the number of properties grew, the need to take on more staff increased. The staff were needed to clean the cottages during the lets and before the next group of people started their stay in a cottage. Bedding had to be changed, and all furniture and equipment checked to make sure it was in working order.

It was vital to have the right staff in place for these tasks. P&J could not afford to hand over a cottage to a new set of customers if it was not really clean and tidy. Any maintenance would also have to be dealt with, which was Perry's responsibility. Supervising the cleaners was done by Ben, an affable man who lacked the toughness to cope with a large number of part-time cleaners who might or might not turn up at the right cottage at the right time. Being too nice, Ben would often just try to do some of the cleaning himself rather than discipline the staff.

Several bookings had recently been lost because cottages had not been cleaned and some damaged kitchen equipment had not been reported as broken and subsequently had not been repaired. Joseph thought it would be necessary to get someone in who would be a lot firmer with the staff. It was, according to Joseph, debatable if P&J could afford to take on more staff.

However, the real problem was that the staff were not well paid and the cleaners did not know which cottage they would be sent to. They also had to fill in several forms about the condition of the cottage, what cleaning they had undertaken and what cleaning materials they had used. Their hours of work had to be registered at the office before going to whichever cottage they were assigned to clean. Although travel costs were paid for, travelling could take a significant amount of time, especially in the peak holiday periods. This travel time was not paid for and caused many of the workers to try to get the cottages nearest to the office. This would often lead to arguments among them.

The only incentive given to the staff was a bonus of £8 if two cottages were cleaned in one morning. It was no wonder that absenteeism was high and that staff were constantly complaining and leaving their job without notice.

In July 2009, Joseph met an old friend, Emily, who had a flat that she wanted to sell as she was moving to London. Joseph thought this would be a different type of property to add to the cottages that the business already owned. If he could get the price right for renting, he thought it might be the start of something big. Unfortunately, by the time Perry had managed to renovate the flat, the economy had taken a serious turn for the worse.

People were cancelling their rentals for the cottages in the summer and the casual weekend bookings started to decline as well. This made renting out the flat for holidays even harder. Joseph thought the best thing to do was to use price skimming as a strategy. He felt that a short-term pricing strategy was right, as in the existing economic climate he might not keep the flat for very long; it would be better to gain a high revenue for a short

period of time. Emily was not so convinced and suggested he think again, especially as a fall in demand would affect the cash flow of the business quite seriously. There were maintenance bills to pay and new staff would need to be recruited to replace those who had recently left.

Joseph did some sums and came up with the idea of charging £595 per week for the flat. However, although it was in a good location, overlooking the lake, it was small and lacked many of the amenities associated with flats in the area. The one bedroom was just big enough for a double bed but little else and the bathroom was also small. He advertised the flat as the perfect getaway for a romantic weekend.

Table 1

Average price level per flat (rent)	£595
Number of lets per year	28
Direct costs (per week)	£50
Overheads (per annum)	£2,700

Questions

Section A

ⓔ It is important not to spend too much time on this section of the paper.

(Question 1 does NOT relate to the case study.)

(1) (a) State two types of business objective. (2 marks)

ⓔ A 'state' question only requires you to state and nothing more. It is very important that you do not waste valuable time offering unnecessary detail. Strategic and tactical objectives are the obvious answers.

(b) State two current liabilities that could appear on a balance sheet. (2 marks)

ⓔ Another 'state' question. You only need to state two examples without explanation. Likely answers are an overdraft, a short-term loan (less than 1 year) and creditors.

(c) Define on-the-job training. (2 marks)

ⓔ 'Define' means just that; however, it would be worthwhile offering an example to enhance your answer. On-the-job training occurs at the place of work and is given either by an outside agency or by the firm's employees.

(d) Calculate the market share of a firm that has sales of £15,000 out of a total market that has increased by £15,000 from £60,000. (4 marks)

ⓔ For all calculations remember to show how you arrive at your answer. In other words, always show your working. Percentage calculations are often badly answered but are regularly examined.

Notice that there is a small task to calculate the actual total market before calculating the firm's share.

$$\text{market share} = \frac{\text{sales of 15,000}}{75,000 \ (60,000 + 15,000)} \times 100 = 20\%$$

Notice how it is obvious what calculations have been undertaken, so if an error was made in the answer, the student would still get 2 or 3 marks.

(e) Outline two styles of leadership.   (4 marks)

For an 'outline' question, remember to ensure that you gain the Level 2 marks available. To do this you need to offer more than a definition; some sort of explanation is required.

Democratic, autocratic or laissez-faire leadership styles can be used (only two are required). Stating what is associated with each style will be sufficient.

(f) Explain two factors that could help improve the cash flow of a business.   (4 marks)

Again, to gain the Level 2 marks, ensure you offer an explanation. Show how your choice actually improves the cash flow of a business.

Possible answers are: selling assets, increasing sales, factoring, leasing, overdrafts, reducing creditor periods to customers, purchasing less stock and holding less stock. For any two of these, try to ensure that you state exactly how the cash flow will be improved. For example, by increasing sales, more revenue will be gained and therefore there will be more current assets (cash).

Total for Section A: 18 marks

Section B

(Questions 2–5 are related to the case study.)

Remember that these questions do relate to the case study and therefore you must use the context of the case to gain Level 3 and 4 marks.

(2) (a) Using the information in Table 1, calculate the total contribution.   (4 marks)

You have been given the figures to use in the table. However, it is still vital to show all your working and state any formula you use.

total contribution = contribution per unit × sales = (price − direct costs) × sales

$$= (£595 − £50) \times 28 = £545 \times 28 = £15,260$$

Although the overheads have been stated, you don't need to calculate the profit as the question does not ask for this.

(b) Discuss how P&J could improve its cash flow. (16 marks)

e The question asks you to discuss and therefore after you have considered the available and appropriate options for how to improve the business's cash flow, you should to try to suggest which would be the most appropriate in the context of the business and its circumstances (Level 4). It is quite legitimate for you to comment on the fact that you have no actual figures so do not know how serious the situation is; therefore your suggestions as to how to improve the cash flow will necessarily be less specific. Although there are several ways in which the cash flow of the business could be improved (increasing sales, selling assets, leasing, purchasing less stock or operating JIT, factoring, reducing credit terms to customers and taking out an overdraft), there is a need to be selective for this business. For example, purchasing less stock is hardly appropriate (apart from cleaning materials) and would not make a great deal of difference. Offering a justified judgement as to which would be the most appropriate method in the present set of circumstances is required if a Level 4 mark is to be gained. Reducing the credit period for payment (e.g. requiring immediate payment rather than payment when the stay begins) may not be a good idea when bookings are falling.

(3) Recommend how P&J could improve the quality of the work undertaken by its cleaning staff. (16 marks)

e The trigger word is 'recommend' and therefore the examiner is looking for a Level 4 answer. It is important to use the context of the case and therefore refer to how P&J could improve the quality of cleaning work. This means you will need to talk about the actual tasks that are undertaken. Remember to avoid general comments about quality control that would apply only to a productive process within a factory. P&J is a service business and therefore quality is related to how clean the cottages are and the state of the equipment within them. It may also be related to how customers are dealt with when booking and arriving at the cottages. References to how the employees report any damage is equally valid. It is also important to try to use the information that you have been given. For example, the economic climate is not favourable and therefore quality becomes even more important. References to training, quality circles, more inspection of work, TQM, or simply increasing employee motivation, are all legitimate answers.

(4) Evaluate the appropriate pricing strategies that P&J could have used for the one-bedroom flat. (16 marks)

e The trigger word 'evaluate' requires a Level 4 response. The justified judgement will come about as a result of considering which pricing strategy is most appropriate for the one-bedroom flat in these circumstances.

Note also the word 'appropriate', suggesting that some strategies for pricing would not be suitable. Using the context of the case is therefore essential.

You are expected to consider the strategy put forward by Joseph, but you do not have to agree with it. You might want to suggest that Joseph is wrong to try for a high price and there are better alternatives. Marginal costing or competitive pricing may be more appropriate, especially in the present economic climate, and some rental income is better than none. Making a contribution to overheads is worthwhile even if profits are limited. Given the size of the flat and Joseph's hope that this may lead to bigger and better things, charging a high price is not really appropriate. However, if it is the intention to sell on very quickly, it might be worth trying to gain a high rent. It is good practice to present a balanced view of both sides of the argument before making a justified judgement as to which is better.

(5) Discuss the most appropriate methods of motivating the company's staff in a more effective manner.

(20 marks)

ⓔ It is important to note that the question asks you to consider the 'most appropriate methods'. It also asks you to think about motivating the staff in a 'more effective manner'. Therefore your answer will need to explain what criteria you are using for 'effective'. Effectiveness might involve being cost-effective, or successfully motivating the staff and helping to improve the quality of their work. It might also mean that the level of absenteeism falls. Therefore when considering the various approaches, you will need to think about how the employees at P&J can be motivated and then try to justify your observations with references to the theories of motivation. A poor answer may just list the theories. A good answer will apply certain selected theories, appropriate for P&J, and show the implications of using them and how they will hopefully improve motivation in an effective way.

Total for Section B: 72 marks

Overall total: 90 marks

Student answer

Section A

(1) **(a)** 2 types of objectives are tactical and strategic.

ⓔ **2/2 marks awarded.** Correct answer, although there is no need to write out part of the question.

(b) Current liabilities are an overdraft and creditors.

ⓔ **2/2 marks awarded.**

(c) On-the-job training takes place whilst at work and is usually done by other employees who have the experience and time.

ⓔ **2/2 marks awarded.** The student has correctly shown that it takes place at work and who does the training. It could be at work by an outside agency as well.

(d) 15,000 × 100 = 20%
     75,000

ⓔ **4/4 marks awarded.** Some workings have been shown. Although the student does not show how the 75,000 was reached, this does not matter provided the sum is correct. A clear layout to help the examiner is to be encouraged.

(e) Two styles of leadership are autocratic and democratic. **a** An autocratic leader makes all the decisions and does not involve the workers. This type of leader is centralised. **b** A democratic leader involves the workers so they are more motivated. **c**

ⓔ **4/4 marks awarded. a** Level 1 marks — the student shows knowledge of leadership styles. **b** This is sufficient to show an understanding, especially the comment on the lack of employee involvement, and would gain Level 2 marks. (The comment on centralisation is on the right lines, but on its own would not have gained Level 2 marks, as it is not clear what the link is between the style of leadership and a centralised organisation.) **c** This is a Level 2 comment. The student offers a link between involvement and motivation.

> **(f)** Two factors that would help improve the cash flow are trying to sell more goods and therefore gain more money. **a** It could also borrow using an overdraft to help it out for a short period of time until sales pick up. This would help meet bills the business has to pay. **b**

ℯ **3/4 marks awarded**. **a** The student has stated one factor but without explaining how this would help the cash flow of the business. This therefore only gains a Level 1 mark. **b** This is a better attempt to explain how borrowing would help. It would therefore get the benefit of doubt and gain a Level 2 mark. It is important to show a clear link between the method suggested and how it will actually improve the cash flow.

ℯ **Total for Section A: 17/18 marks**

Section B

(2) **(a)** Total contribution = contribution per unit × sales **a**
$$= 555 × 28 = £15,540 \textbf{ b}$$

ℯ **1/4 marks awarded. a** 1 mark for showing the formula, although a second mark was not gained because the student did not show how contribution per unit is calculated (contribution per unit = price − direct costs). **b** This is a classic example of why it is so important to show your working. The figure £555 is incorrect and, although it is multiplied by the right figure, the final answer is therefore wrong. However, students do not get penalised twice for a mistake and the own figure rule applies. Therefore, if you show your workings and you make a mistake, marks can still be awarded for the correct method. The answer should be (£595 − 50) × 28 = £545 × 28 = £15,260.

> **(b)** The cash flow of P&J could be improved if it dropped its prices. **a** By doing this it might sell more cottages for rent and therefore increase the revenue for the business. **b** P&J could also borrow from the bank by getting an overdraft. **c** This could be used to help pay the wages of the cleaners or maintenance bills until more cash came into the business from the rents, therefore reducing the problem of a negative cash flow. **d** The problem for the business is that this would cost them **e** money because they would have to pay interest on the overdraft which would actually add to their costs, something they don't want in these economic circumstances. **f** Another way to improve the cash flow of the business is to buy less stock as this would mean less money is flowing out of the business. **g**
>
> But for P&J the amount of money saved would not be very much and it is very important that the cleaning stuff is there as this is an important part of the image of the business. **h** To evaluate, I think the best way to improve the cash flow of the business would be the dropping of the prices as this would increase sales revenue. **i**

ℯ **11/16 marks awarded.** Note that in this case, the student did not label the answer clearly — this has been corrected here to avoid confusion. It may appear a minor issue, but now that scripts are scanned electronically, it is essential to number questions clearly.

a A Level 1 mark for the correct knowledge of a way to improve cash flow. **b** This is Level 2 but no higher, as there is no link as to its effect on the cash flow of P&J. The explanation is just sufficient for a Level 2 mark. **c** Another Level 1 statement of a possible way to improve the cash flow. **d** An obvious implication for the business is given, but it would have been better if the student had clearly shown how it would improve the cash flow. This would probably just about reach a Level 3 mark as an attempt at analysis. **e** Try to remember that a business is singular and therefore should be called by its name (P&J) or 'it'. **f** This is clear analysis, highlighting the implication for the business in an effective manner. It would therefore gain a Level 3 mark. **g** This is another possible route to improving the cash flow of the business (Level 1). **h** This is a good implication for the business, as it suggests that this particular option for improving the cash flow would not be appropriate. There is the start of a judgement (Level 4), but it lacks justification at this point. Nevertheless a clear Level 3 mark would be gained. **i** Just because a student writes 'to evaluate', it does not mean that Level 4 marks will be awarded. It is necessary to offer a justified judgement. No suggestion is offered for why a particular method of solving the cash-flow problem will be better than another for this business in these circumstances, and therefore a Level 4 mark is missed. Nevertheless, a good Level 3 mark would be gained.

(3) The quality of the work done by the cleaners could be improved by firstly paying them a better wage. **a** Taylor **b** thought that people like more money and that's what motivates them and even if it does not actually motivate them it might stop them rushing and therefore they might do the job to a better standard. They could also offer a better incentive to clean more than one cottage, but that might encourage the cleaners to hurry and therefore not do the job properly which would mean that the customers would not book again if the cottage was not really clean. **c**

They could introduce quality circles **d** which is when the employees are allowed to discuss problems at work in work time and solve the problems, especially for the incentives to clean more than one cottage and who is sent to which cottage. **e** They might decide that the cleaners could go straight to the cottage and not have to go to the office first and this would be a sense of involvement which is something Mayo **f** said was important to motivate the workers. If they are motivated they will work to a better standard and the quality of cleaning will improve. **g**

Hertzberg suggested that the hygiene factors frustrate workers. The work, paperwork and systems frustrate workers and they may not concentrate on the quality of their work. But if jobs were rotated it would give job enrichment, a motivator according to Hertzberg, and therefore the quality of the work should improve. **h**

Allowing the workers to be involved by having the quality circles would be the best idea even though they would still all have to go to the office which annoys them. If they could see that their views are important and are allowed to help decide the best way to organise the cleaning of the cottages and be allowed to go straight to the cottages it would also give them more responsibility which would motivate them and therefore the quality of the cleaning may improve. It will depend on how good Ben is and this is a problem but he would not have to discipline them as they would be happier. It may also save the business money by not having to get someone else in and therefore adding to the costs of the business. **i**

P and J could also apply a system of TQM. **j**

ⓔ **14/16 marks awarded. a** Level 1 knowledge. This is then supported by **b**. **b** Using the name of a theorist is a good idea. The answer explains what Taylor states (Level 2). **c** Analysis attempting to show the implication for the business in terms of quality. **d** Reference to a business studies concept (Level 1). **e** Level 2 comment is made as the concept of quality circles is explained. **f** Another Level 2 comment with appropriate use of a theorist. **g** A linked comment about the effects of being involved on the quality of the work is analysis, though only just, and therefore achieves Level 3. **h** This is a well-written comment. The name of a theorist (which is incorrectly spelt — it should be Herzberg) is used and explained, and the implications for the quality of the work are shown clearly. Consequently, this would gain a good Level 3 mark. **i** This last paragraph is a really good piece of evaluation (Level 4). The student has made a judgement about which would be the best way to improve the quality of the work undertaken. The view is justified in the context of the case, and an understanding of the significance of Ben is brought in to good effect. **j** Another piece of knowledge on quality (Level 1).

(4) It was not a good idea to charge a high price for the flat, especially when we are told that the number of people taking weekend breaks is declining and people are cancelling bookings. **a** If Joseph is hoping the flat would be the start of something big then he would be better to start with penetration pricing **b** and therefore start with a low price in order to gain a part of the market first. **c** Once he has gained a share of the market he can increase his prices, assuming he has got some customer loyalty and therefore they will be prepared to pay a higher price for something they like and want to return to. However we are told that the flat is very small and therefore he needs to charge less as otherwise people will be expecting something better for a higher price and will be very disappointed and therefore not come back again. They might even tell other friends and family that it is not worth it and this will damage the reputation of P&J and could affect future sales. **d**

He could also try using promotional pricing. **e** This can be used for a short time as a form of advertising — for example the first three bookings get a 20% price cut. This will encourage people to come and try the flat and if they like it they can tell other people and this will lead to other bookings and increase Joseph's revenue. **f** He might also think about a psychological price of £499 as this sounds a lot less and therefore might help increase demand.

Whichever pricing strategy he uses, he has to try and get people to come and try the flat. They will want value for money and therefore I think he should charge a lower price and use a mixture of promotional and penetration pricing. By charging a lower price without worrying people that it is too cheap, he is more likely to get people to stay because they will be able to afford it, even when the number of bookings is falling because of the economic circumstances. This should actually lead to more revenue than if he had charged a higher price because there will be more people coming again. **g**

ⓔ **15/16 marks awarded. a** This is a Level 2 comment. There is an explanation of why charging a high price is not appropriate. **b** A pricing strategy — this shows knowledge and is therefore Level 1. **c** An explanation of penetration pricing (Level 2). **d** An implication for the business of setting a high price in the context of the case (Level 3). **e** Another example of the student's knowledge of pricing strategies (Level 1). **f** Sufficient for Level 3 marks, as the student has shown how the strategy would affect the business. **g** A justified judgement is made and therefore this is effective evaluation in the context of the case.

(5) P&J need to encourage the workers to take on more responsibility. To do this the owners need to allow the workers the opportunity to have the responsibility. Empowerment is a good way to do this. **a** The workers can decide when to do a particular cottage and how it is done. **b** This will give them a lot of responsibility and the workers are more likely to feel motivated and therefore perform the tasks to a higher standard. This will mean that the customers who rent the cottages will be satisfied and come again. **c** Because the workers would be allowed to take the responsibility for who does which cottage and when, this fits Hertzberg's **d** theory about motivators.

Another method to help motivate the workers at P&J would be to use job rotation. **e** This could be done by ensuring that the same workers do not have to clean the same cottage every time. This variety would make the workers happier as they will have a change of work and therefore avoid getting bored. However, it may be better for the workers to have the responsibility for particular cottages so they get a sense of belonging and ownership and will then take pride in keeping their cottage nice and clean. **f** Another important factor for P&J to think about is the cost of implementing any of these methods to improve the motivation of the workers. Although it might cost more to operate job enrichment or job rotation, it might be worthwhile if they are more motivated and therefore revenue is gained from extra rents because the cottages look good and are nice and clean. **g**

P&J could offer an incentive to the workers by having a profit sharing scheme or a prize incentive. The worker who cleans a particular cottage and gets any comments about how clean it is from the people renting it could gain points and the worker with the most points would win a prize. The trouble with this idea is that particular cottages might be easier to clean or the workers would not be able to clean as many because they are working really hard on one. This would not help P&J as they need all the cottages cleaned ready for the next customers. **h**

ⓔ **17/20 marks awarded. a** These opening sentences are at Level 2. The correct term, 'responsibility', is used (Level 1) and the explanation is clear (Level 2). **b** This brief explanation of empowerment is a Level 2 comment. **c** This is clear analysis. There is an implication for the business in the context of the case. **d** It is a good approach to use a theorist to explain what you are saying (although Herzberg is still spelt incorrectly). However, the theory could have been explained more thoroughly in order to gain additional marks. **e** Reference to job rotation is knowledge (Level 1). **f** This section is of interest. The student has offered some analysis (Level 3) of the consequences of using job rotation, but has also offered a judgement as to the alternative consequences. However, there is probably insufficient justification to gain a Level 4 mark at this stage. **g** This is a justified judgement as to the alternatives in terms of costs and benefits of job rotation or job enrichment, and consequently would gain a low Level 4 mark. **h** This is another example where the student has offered a balanced view of the advantages and disadvantages, and has then made a judgement as to which is the best. It would therefore gain a Level 4 mark.

This answer is unusual in that it deservedly gains a Level 4 mark without actually opting for which method is the best in terms of motivating staff. The student has made several judgements and would be rewarded accordingly.

Total for Section B: 58/72 marks

Overall total: 75/90 marks — a good A grade

Case study 2 **The Cornflower Cupcake Company**

2 hours

Mary Grocott started her business, the Cornflower Cupcake Company (CCC), almost by chance, 12 years ago. She had two young children who occupied most of her time, but she had always enjoyed baking. At about that time, there was a big interest in cupcakes, which was an American confectionery that had not often been seen in the UK. Having watched television chefs produce them, Mary decided to have a go. She started by selling her cupcakes to friends and family and at local markets and fêtes. They generated a great deal of interest and customers began to ask Mary if she could customise her cakes and make special orders for them. Seeing a gap in the market, Mary decided to go into it as a business venture rather than a hobby, to make a bit of extra money.

Mary quickly moved from her own kitchen to an industrial unit on a nearby business park and began to produce on a much larger scale. Most of her business still came from personal recommendation, but she also created a website and started to send her cupcakes out to customers through delivery firms and the post. In addition, Mary approached national and local magazines and asked them if they would like to do a feature on her cupcakes. She has never paid for promotion apart from this.

Mary wonders whether she should undertake some market research to see if there are opportunities that she is missing. She is interested in expanding, but unsure of the best way to proceed with this.

Mary now employs 18 full-time and 20 part-time workers producing cupcakes, as well as a finance manager, Tony, who handles wages and the recruitment of new workers. Mary deals with all the marketing aspects of the business and oversees the production line, with the help of her supervisor, Jane.

In recent weeks, Jane has been discussing staff turnover problems with Mary (see Appendix 1). Apart from some of the workers who have been with Mary from the outset, staff turnover is very high. Most of the workers are either straight from school or are women with young children. Jane feels that they have two problems. The first is that there is insufficient time to give the young workers adequate training. As a consequence, they tend to remain in the unskilled and routine jobs for long periods and see little hope of advancement. The second problem is that the women with young children want to be able to choose their hours. Most want to work part time from 10 a.m. to 3 p.m. so that their job fits in with school hours. This puts extra pressure on those workers who work a normal 8-hour day. Jane thinks that Mary needs to address these issues.

To add to this, Mary has recently been approached by a national supermarket that sells at the higher end of the market. It wants to start to sell a specialist range of Mary's cupcakes in their larger stores, with a view to selling throughout the chain eventually. Mary could not handle the business without taking on extra staff and moving to a new site. She has investigated the possibility of taking the available unit next to her. Tony has calculated figures for the investment in new equipment that would be required (see Appendix 2). Mary knows that she and Tony need to sit down and do an investment appraisal on these figures to see if the contract is worth considering.

Mary has also experienced problems over the years with stock control. Most of the stock that the business uses is either perishable or has short use-by dates. Mary feels that there is far too much waste because new stock is simply piled on top of what is there already. In addition, there is a lack of space if more than one delivery comes within a day. This means that stock then has to be stored in the production area. Mary wishes that she had the time to investigate the alternatives available to her to manage this situation better.

Mary is beginning to realise that she is taking too much responsibility for the day-to-day running of the business. She is wondering if she should employ more staff with middle management roles so that she has more time to address all the issues that arise and to consider the future direction of the business.

Appendix 1 Employee information

Number of employees as at 31/12/12: 18 full time; 20 part time working 50% of the week

Full-time equivalent employees: 28

Staff leaving information for 2012

Name	Start date	Leaving date	Job area	Reason for leaving	Part/full
Holly Davis	02/04/2012	04/07/2012	Bakery	Childcare problems	Full
Daisy Matthews	19/08/2011	31/08/2012	Decorating	New job with better prospects	Full
Nadia Matin	24/07/2011	30/09/2012	Despatch	Job was boring	Full
India Nagi	04/01/2012	07/07/2012	Bakery	Childcare problems	Full
James Evans	07/07/2011	08/06/2012	Bakery	No prospects	Full
Ruth Martin	08/08/2011	02/04/2012	Bakery	New job	Full
Karen Webb	06/07/2011	02/03/2012	Decorating	No prospects	Full

Appendix 2 Financial information for the proposed new unit and supermarket contract

The cost of taking out a 5-year lease on the unit and equipping it is £30,000.

Net cash inflows from the order are forecast as follows:

Year	Net cash inflow
0	(20,000)
1	12,000
2	12,000
3	12,000
4	14,000
5	15,000

Appendix 3 Review article

The following article featured in *Amazing Family Food* magazine (June 2009).

Cornflower Cupcakes

We tried these delicious cupcakes when they were delivered to one of the office staff as a birthday surprise and we can definitely recommend them. They are produced by Mary Grocott and her team in a small factory in the Midlands and each one is hand decorated and finished.

The only way to buy Cornflower Cupcakes at the moment is to order them online or by phone, direct from the business. They will then be delivered to you — or anyone else you choose — by next-day delivery. They can be customised by colour or design if you wish

and they all arrive beautifully packed in a cornflower-blue gift box. They make a lovely change from a traditional birthday cake.

Questions

Section A

ⓔ It is important not to spend too much time on this part of the paper.

(Question 1 does NOT relate to the case study.)

(1) (a) Give examples of two methods of market segmentation. (2 marks)

ⓔ This question only requires you to give two examples and nothing more. It is important not to waste time putting in too much detail.

(b) State two leadership styles. (2 marks)

ⓔ Once again, simply state two examples without further explanation.

(c) Define the breakeven point for a business. (2 marks)

ⓔ 'Define' means just that, although it would be a good idea to give an example to ensure that you gain both marks.

(d) A business finds that, when it increases the price of one of its products from £4 to £5, the demand falls from 1,000 to 900. Calculate the price elasticity of demand. (4 marks)

ⓔ As in all calculations, it is important to show your working. It is also a good idea to start off by giving the formula. If you make a mistake in your calculation, you will then still be given the credit for using the correct method.

(e) Explain two benefits that will come from total quality management. (4 marks)

ⓔ If the trigger word is 'explain', you need to ensure that you put in further detail and don't just state the benefits. There will be Level 2 marks to gain. In answer to this question, give the benefit and then explain how the firm might lower costs, raise productivity or increase sales as a consequence.

(f) Outline two methods of below-the-line promotion. (4 marks)

ⓔ An 'outline' question also needs further explanation to gain the Level 2 marks. In this question you should give the example of a promotion method. You should then explain what the particular benefits of this system are and how it could be used to increase sales.

Total for Section A: 18 marks

Section B

(Questions 2–5 are related to the case study.)

ⓔ Remember that these questions relate to the case study and it is important to write in context if you are to achieve Level 3 or 4 marks.

(2) (a) Using the information provided, calculate the labour turnover for the Cornflower Cupcake Company (CCC) in 2012. (4 marks)

ⓔ You have been given the figures required to calculate the labour turnover. It is important to remember to show all your working and to begin by giving the formula. All of this will help you to gain marks and ensure that you still achieve some credit, even if you make a silly mistake in the calculation.

The formula you need is that labour turnover is the number of workers leaving as a percentage of the total workforce. Show this first before giving the calculation.

(b) With reference to the case study, recommend ways in which Mary could reduce labour turnover at CCC. (16 marks)

ⓔ The trigger word in this question is 'recommend'. This means that the examiner is looking for a Level 4 answer to the question. It is important, therefore, to write in the context of the case and to ensure that you eventually come to a point where you can make a recommendation and justify it.

You should begin by discussing two or three ways in which Mary can reduce labour turnover. These may be methods to do with payment, with motivation or with flexible working. In each case, you should explain the benefits of following a particular course of action. It is very important not to write a long list of points that are at Level 2 and never go on to analyse the particular benefits to Mary and the business. However many points you make at Level 2, you will never achieve the Level 3 or 4 marks unless you analyse them.

Finally, to achieve Level 4 marks, you must weigh up your suggestions and make a recommendation to Mary. Remember that there are no right or wrong answers. As long as you can justify your answer effectively, it will be valid.

(3) Discuss the methods that Mary could use to improve the system of stock control at CCC. (16 marks)

ⓔ The trigger word in this question is 'discuss'. This means that, to achieve Level 4, you need to come to a conclusion about the best way for Mary to improve stock control. There are several ways in which stock control can be improved. You could discuss the advantages and disadvantages of just-in-time ordering. You could also discuss the particular problems for a business like Mary's in relying on suppliers to restock daily. The uncertainty of demand is an issue here.

At the end of your answer, you must ensure that you suggest the best way to proceed. This might involve Mary using a combination of different methods to deal with stock control problems in her specific business.

(4) Using the information given, recommend whether Mary should proceed with the contract with the supermarket. (16 marks)

ⓔ It is possible to answer this question well without using calculations, but if you want to achieve Level 3 marks quickly and easily, it is always better to use the figures. The question can be answered by discussing the changes in Mary's lifestyle and the work involved in taking on the contract with the supermarket. The correct use of investment appraisal will mean that the answer automatically achieves Level 3 marks. It would be possible to use either ARR or payback or to use both and compare their relative merits. It is also important to point out that neither method is perfect and that both have problems associated with them.

Having discussed the investment appraisal methods, it would then be useful to mention the problems that Mary might encounter if her business grows. She might lose day-to-day control and she might need to employ many more staff.

At the end, you must come to a conclusion about whether the contract should be accepted or not, and this must be justified. Once again, there is no right or wrong answer. Whatever the financial information shows, it is up to you to persuade the examiner with your arguments.

(5) Evaluate the methods of market research that Mary might use in looking at opportunities for expansion. (20 marks)

ⓔ The trigger word here is 'evaluate', so this should also be a Level 4 answer. It is important that you finish your answer with a list of suggestions for Mary in terms of market research and that they are justified in terms of cost and appropriateness. Do not try to discuss too many alternatives. The obvious way to proceed is to consider collecting information from current customers and from prospective customers. At each point you must weigh up how much Mary can afford to do, given that this is a small business with limited resources. Paying external agencies for market research may give better results, but they come at a cost. Try to think of cheaper and easier ways to access customers in order to gain their opinions. One way would be to use an online questionnaire when an order is placed.

Having done this and analysed your alternatives, you must then suggest the way you think Mary should proceed in order to find the information she needs to ensure that her business is successful.

Total for Section B: 72 marks

Overall total: 90 marks

Student answer

Section A

(1) (a) Age   Gender

ⓔ **2/2 marks awarded.** The student has given two acceptable answers. There is no need for further clarification to gain full marks.

(b) Democratic   Autocratic

ⓔ **2/2 marks awarded.** The student has stated two leadership styles correctly.

(c) Breakeven point is the level of output where the revenue from sales exactly covers the fixed and variable costs of production. No profit is made.

ⓔ **2/2 marks awarded.** This is a correct definition.

> **(d)** elasticity of demand $= \dfrac{\% \text{ change in } Q}{\% \text{ change in } P}$
>
> $\% \text{ change in } Q = \dfrac{100}{1,000} \times 100 = 10\%$ ✓
>
> $\% \text{ change in } P = \dfrac{1}{4} \times 100 = 25\%$ ✓
>
> elasticity $\quad = \dfrac{10}{25}$ ✓ $= 0.4$ ✓

ⓔ **4/4 marks awarded.** The student has gone through each stage of the calculation, showing all the working in full (marks for each stage are shown by ✓). It is important to show the working in case an error is made. In this case all the calculations are correct.

> **(e)** Total quality management means ensuring that quality is the responsibility of every member of the workforce. If a firm uses TQM it will mean that there will be less waste because faults will be found sooner so this will save money for the business. **a** It will also mean that the business does not need to employ quality control checkers for the finished goods which will also reduce costs of production. **b**

ⓔ **4/4 marks awarded. a** The student gives an explanation of a cost saving which will benefit the business (Level 2). **b** A further acceptable cost saving is given (also Level 2).

> **(f)** Below-the-line promotion is using promotional methods that are not in the mass media. Two examples would be personal selling and trade fairs.

ⓔ **2/4 marks awarded.** In this answer the student has only stated, rather than outlined with more detail. The answer should have given a brief explanation of each of the promotional methods.

Total for Section A: 16/18 marks

Section B

> **(2) (a)** labour turnover $= \dfrac{\text{number of workers leaving}}{\text{total number of employees}} \times 100$ ✓
>
> labour turnover for 2012 $= \dfrac{7}{28} \times 100$ ✓ $= 25\%$ ✓

ⓔ **4/4 marks awarded.** Working is shown and the calculation is correct.

> **(b)** The labour turnover for CCC is high for a manufacturing business and it will be imposing costs on the firm in terms of recruitment of new workers and training them to do the job.

Mary has been told that there is a problem by her supervisor. The two problems need approaching in different ways, although the outcome should be that Mary manages to keep her workers for longer and they should be happier in their work.

First of all Mary needs to do something about training her workers and ensuring that they are not bored or unappreciated. She should appoint one of her more senior and established workers as a training officer. **a** They should be given the responsibility for the induction of new staff and then their ongoing training. All workers should be given regular training sessions and also given the opportunity to transfer to another sector of the business if necessary.

It might also help if the whole workforce was given regular training and teambuilding sessions. Together with staff social activities, this could make workers feel part of a team and valued members of the business. Mary needs her workers to know that she appreciates what they do. If these things are well received, Mary could build up a loyal group of employees who are proud to work for a successful firm. This could result in not only lower labour turnover, but greater efficiency and higher turnover in the long run. **b**

Mary could also think about using some sort of a bonus or profit sharing system as well that is dependent on the length of service. If workers stayed for at least a year and had regular attendance, they could then go into the scheme. Catering is a sector with high labour turnover so Mary needs to do all she can to keep good workers. **c**

As far as the problems with workers with children are concerned, the first thing Mary should do is to discuss the problems with them. She needs to find out what their difficulties are and whether the firm can work around them so that both sides are happy. Mary already employs some part-time workers so it must be possible to offer this as an alternative. **d**

It is possible that some sort of job-share system might help those workers who are having problems. At the moment it seems that Mary is ignoring the issue and letting workers leave. This is a waste of valuable resources if the workers who are leaving are trained and good at their job. Mary needs to think about what she is prepared to do to ensure that she keeps good employees. At the end of the day, they are vital in ensuring the success of the business.

In the short term Mary either needs to address these HR problems herself or give the responsibility for HR to someone else. She needs to realise that her employees are important and that she is wasting time and money in constantly having to replace those who leave. In the long term a happier and more productive workforce will be worth the expense of sorting out these problems. **e**

ⓔ **13/16 marks awarded. a** The student is showing that he/she understands the problems, by explaining their effects on the business. The answer then goes on to give some of the solutions that Mary might use. This would achieve Level 2 marks. **b** The student is giving a range of alternative solutions to the problems of high labour turnover at the business. This would take the answer to the top of Level 2. **c** At this point, the answer moves into an analysis of the results of implementing the suggested solutions at CCC. This would achieve Level 3 marks. **d** This is a further point at Level 2. **e** The answer achieves some level of evaluation here by saying that addressing the problem in the short term would bring long-term benefits. Another way of achieving Level 4 marks would be to discuss the best solutions to the problem.

(3) At the present time, Mary does not really have a system of stock control. The result of not having a stock control system is wastage, higher costs per unit of output and general disorganisation. **a**

The product produced by CCC uses raw materials that are perishable and need to be stored in cool or refrigerated conditions. This means that they will be expensive to store and could go off quickly. The obvious method for Mary to use is one of just-in-time (JIT) stock ordering. In this sort of system, raw materials are delivered on a regular basis as and when they are needed. This can mean that the business carries no stocks of raw materials at all **b** This would have all sorts of advantages for Mary. She would not have to take up valuable space with the ingredients for the cupcakes and she would not have to pay the cost of storage for them.

The advantages of this system would be lower costs for the firm in all stock areas and this would therefore lower the firm's costs per unit and give them the chance to make higher profits. **c**

The problem with JIT stock control is that the business needs to have a reliable supplier and to take deliveries on a regular basis. It can also mean that the business loses economies of scale by not being able to order in bulk.

I would suggest that Mary uses JIT alongside keeping a limited amount of back-up stock in case any last minute orders come in. **d** She could order ingredients on a daily basis, but always keep a small supply in stock for emergencies. She also needs to ensure that she uses stock rotation with any stock she holds. This means that she puts any new stock to the back and takes out older stocks for use first.

Using this combination should mean that Mary has less money tied up in stock, that she wastes less and that she does not use valuable space with huge amounts of perishable stock.

ⓔ **12/16 marks awarded. a** The student understands the problems of stock control and gives examples of the costs. **b** The answer goes on to discuss the alternatives open to Mary, explaining how the JIT system would work and its benefits. **c** The answer then goes on to analyse the benefits for the business in terms of lower costs and compares these to the problems of introducing and using JIT systems for a business. This would achieve Level 3 marks. **d** Finally the answer makes a recommendation for the business that might help overcome the present stock control problems.

A higher mark could have been achieved in this question by comparing JIT with alternative stock control systems more directly.

(4) Mary and Tony could use some sort of investment appraisal to show whether it is worth accepting the order from the supermarket.

If they used the payback they would look at the returns to determine how long it would take to pay back the original investment. **a** The outlay is £30,000. After 2 years the returns will have paid back £24,000, so the contract will pay back during the third year. It will be exactly 2 years and 6 months if the returns are evenly spread. **b**

Payback is a useful measure to use because it will give Mary some idea of the risk she is taking. In this case, just over 2 years is not too big a risk and it is possible that there may be other and bigger contracts as well if everything works out. The problem with payback is that it does not measure profitability and it makes assumptions about when the money comes in. **c**

An alternative would be to use accounting rate of return (ARR). This method uses profit to calculate the average rate of return. Tony could then compare this with profitability elsewhere in the business. In this case the return over the period of 5 years is £65,000. This gives a profit of £35,000. The profit per year is £5,000 and the ARR is 5,000/30,000 which is 16.7%.

This might be the better method to use because it takes all the years of the contract into account and it makes comparisons with other parts of Cornflower Cupcakes possible. For example, if the rest of the business is already earning a return of more than 20%, Tony may advise Mary not to accept the contract. **d** It will depend on whether Mary wants to expand and whether she would like to gain a contract with a large supermarket.

Apart from the financial aspects of the contract, Mary needs to consider very carefully where she wants her business to go in the future. The supermarket contract will change the nature of Mary's business. It will make it much bigger and it may mean that Mary needs to hand over a lot of the day-to-day control. If she wants to keep the business as her own, under her control and to ensure her current lifestyle she may decide to turn down the contract — whatever the profits and business it brings. **e**

I would advise Mary to think very carefully before she accepts this contract. It may bring her success and more money, but it will also bring more work and change the nature of the business. She needs to be sure what she wants before she proceeds.

ⓔ 14/16 marks awarded. a The student understands the use of investment appraisal (Level 1). **b** The answer then makes correct use of the financial information given, by showing calculations for payback and, later, ARR. The answer also explains the advantages and disadvantages of payback. This would take the student to Level 3. **c** The explanation of ARR is also a Level 3 response, making correct use of the information in the case study. **d** The answer evaluates Mary's alternatives, bringing in other factors apart from the financial information. This shows that the student has understood that the decision to expand is not just about profit. This will take the answer to Level 4. **e** The student then goes on to state what the recommendations to Mary would be and gives further evaluation of the situation.

(5) If Mary wishes to expand her business it would be a good idea to do some market research before she starts. The obvious place to start is with her existing customers. **a**

Mary needs to decide whether she is going to do the research herself or whether she should employ a market research company. The advantage of doing it herself is that it will be cheaper. **b** Mary is unlikely to have a large budget available to do this research and market research companies will be very expensive. On the other hand, Mary has little expertise in this area and she is unlikely to know the problems involved in doing market research or how to go about it. **c** This may affect the quality of the information she collects and how useful it is to her. Mary needs to weigh up these alternatives before she proceeds.

Mary sells her cupcakes direct to the customer. This gives her an ideal opportunity to do market research with them. She could put a questionnaire on her website and ask a similar questionnaire of telephone customers. From this she could find out how the customer heard of her, whether they would like her to sell other products and if they would be interested in buying her cupcakes through supermarkets. **c** This would be fairly cheap to do and would give Mary some instant feedback.

However, if Mary wants to expand into new and different areas, she may find it difficult to do the research herself. How would she know who to ask and how to get in touch with people? In this case it might be better to use a specialist market research company, but this would be expensive. **d**

I think that, given the nature and size of the business, Mary should start off by approaching her existing customers with an online survey. I would suggest that she gets a market research firm to help her to compile this survey. **e** From this she will be able to get an idea of her market segment, customer satisfaction and the interest of her customers in other products. She could also find out the best way to market and distribute her products.

ⓔ 15/20 marks awarded. a The answer begins by showing that the student understands the relevance of doing market research (Level 1). **b** The student explains how the problem of available finance will have an impact on what Mary can do. This takes the answer to Level 2. **c** The student then analyses the benefits of using one particular method, taking the answer to low Level 3. **d** The student analyses the pros and cons of doing the work in-house or using a specialist firm. This is further Level 3 discussion. **e** At this point the student evaluates the alternatives (Level 4) and makes a suggestion about the way in which Mary could proceed to get the best results, bearing in mind the financial constraints.

Total for Section B: 58/72 marks

Overall total: 74/90 marks — an A grade

Knowledge check answers

1 Marketing can help a business by:
- identifying markets
- suggesting the right price for a product
- getting the right packaging
- promoting the product
- collecting market research

2 Businesses that are product orientated are:
- usually high tech
- involved in research
- change the specification of the product frequently, e.g. Dyson

3 A holiday firm might segment by age to collect market research information.

4 Market share is the percentage of the total market controlled by a given business, whereas market growth refers to the increase in sales by value or volume.

5 Example of an extension strategy: offering additional features for the same price on an existing model of a car to extend its life.

6 A 'problem child' is sold in an expanding market, therefore it has potential.

7 Price discrimination by time examples include: train franchises such as Virgin, British Gas, BT, O2, Thomson holidays.

8 Channels of distribution have become more direct due to increased use of the internet and a reduction in the role of the wholesaler.

9 Above-the-line promotion includes: television adverts, newspaper and magazine advertising and cinema advertising.

10 Characteristics of products with inelastic demand include:
- few or no substitutes
- necessities
- take a small proportion of consumer income

11 Functions of a budget include:
- progress check
- control of expenditure
- aid to efficiency
- a target
- allows a department to take control of its own budgets

12 Possible causes of cash-flow problems include:
- poor economic climate
- seasonal demand for product/service
- too much stock
- late payments by debtors
- too many debtors
- offering too much credit
- taxation

13 Formula for unit cost = total costs divided by output

14 Examples of social costs include: pollution (air and noise) and congestion (for car usage)

15 Formula for contribution per unit = price − direct costs

16 Formula for total contribution = contribution per unit × sales

17 Profit = price of £15 − direct costs of £4 = £11 × sales of 35 = £385 − overheads of £250 = £135

18 Formula for breakeven = fixed costs divided by contribution per unit

19 Margin of safety = actual output − breakeven output = 2,100 − 1,950 margin of safety = 150(+)

20 Payback measures degree of risk.

21 Limitations of payback include:
- It does not consider the value of money over time.
- It does not take account of any cash inflows after the payback period.
- It does not measure profitability.
- It does not show exactly when cash inflows occur.

22 Benefits of using ARR include:
- It measures profitability.
- It counts all cash flows over the life of the investment.

23 Trading period is the profit/loss made within a given period of time, usually 1 year.

24 Stakeholders that may benefit include: bank, shareholders/investors, potential suppliers, HMRC.

25 The three components of current assets are debtors, stock and cash.

26 Net current assets = current assets − current liabilities

27 Interested stakeholders include: banks (lending), suppliers and potential investors/shareholders.

28 The higher the level of labour turnover, the more likely it is that employee motivation is poor since (for whatever reasons) a large number of employees are leaving.

29 Possible benefits include:
- When employees leave and are replaced this can bring new ideas and new skills to a firm.
- Labour turnover can also be a way to reduce the workforce without redundancies.

30 Possible effects include: high labour turnover, absenteeism, poor productivity, poor quality output and poor industrial relations.

31 Indicators such as absenteeism, productivity and labour turnover are used to analyse if the workforce is 'happy', i.e. motivated. If they are not, they are likely to take days off, produce at a standard below their potential, and eventually leave.

32 Factors to be considered include whether:
- it is possible to measure output and effort accurately
- the scheme will bring envy and resentment and discourage teamworking
- the financial incentives on offer are sufficient to motivate — if a bonus becomes 'part of the norm' it fails to motivate

33 Characteristics of a poor leader include:
- makes all decisions with no employee consultation
- consults employees but then ignores their suggestions
- is not interested in employee suggestions
- adopts an 'I know best' attitude
- is inaccessible
- always seeks to blame others for own mistakes
- does not encourage a sense of belonging

- regards all employees as lazy and therefore needing a theory X management approach at all times

34 Organistic structure: flat structure should mean faster, more effective communication. Democratic style and delegation will hopefully aid motivation. However, a wide span of control may mean a manager is overworked.

Mechanistic structure: leadership is less democratic and so decisions can be made faster. However, the number of layers in the organisation may bring communication problems. Also the small span of control may limit opportunities to delegate.

Centralised structure: autocratic style and limited delegation means decisions can be made quickly. Decisions are made at head office by those best placed to make them. Common policies on issues such as marketing reduce the duplication of resources. However, the limited scope for employee empowerment could affect motivation adversely.

Decentralised structure: decisions (e.g. on prices and wages) are made at a local level and take account of local conditions. Democratic style of leadership and delegation will hopefully aid motivation. However, there can be inconsistencies (e.g. on pay) in the way each branch operates which can cause resentment and confusion.

35 Span of control refers to the number of employees a particular manager is responsible for. The levels of hierarchy describe the number of layers within a business's structure.

36 Possible reasons include:
- Prices had been lowered to generate the sales and if costs stayed the same profit per unit will have fallen.
- If the increase in sales is not significant the overall profit level may fall.
- Unit costs may have risen, e.g. rising labour, marketing and distribution costs.

- More capital equipment may have had to be purchased to produce more units.

37 Capacity utilisation = current output divided by potential output × 100

38 Total costs = fixed costs + variable costs
Unit costs = total costs/output

39 Factors include: the type of product, the demand for the product, the size of the firm, the funds available to the firm, the availability of suitable capital equipment and technology.

40 Characteristics include: less stock, adaptable production, inbuilt defect prevention, skilled employees.

41 Factors to consider include: Who will participate? (Will all employees be involved?) Will meetings take place in work time? (in which case production time is lost) How often will they occur? Will employees actually want to participate? Will employees be rewarded for 'good' suggestions? Employees may become demotivated if their suggestions are not implemented.

42 Reasons include:
- Too much stock ties up capital, involves storage costs, and runs the risk that stock becomes obsolete, damaged or stolen.
- Too little stock can mean production problems and the risk of disappointing a customer.

43 Advantages of quality assurance include:
- saves money— less waste
- better product — more customer satisfaction
- involves workers — motivates

44 Benefits of JIT stock control include:
- less money spent on holding stock
- less money tied up in stock
- cuts waste through poor storage and theft